PENGUIN REFERENCE

THE STATE OF CHINA ATLAS

Robert Benewick is Research Professor of Politics at the University of Sussex. He is the author of numerous publications on politics and on China, including *China in the 1990s* (edited with Paul Wingrove). The recipient of a Leverhulme Emeritus Fellowship, he is currently researching rural and urban governance in China.

Stephanie Donald is a lecturer in Media Studies at Murdoch University, Western Australia. She has previously worked as a Research Fellow in Chinese at the University of Westminster, and has taught Media Studies at the University of Sussex. Her publications include *Picturing Power in the PRC: Posters of the Cultural Revolution* (co-edited with Harriet Evans), and *Public Secrets, Public Spaces: Cinema and Civility in China.*

Robert Benewick and Stephanie Donald are co-editors of *Belief in China: Art and Politics; Deities and Mortality.*

Also in this series:

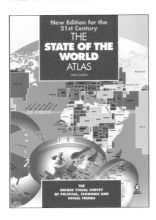

THE STATE OF THE WORLD ATLAS
sixth edition
by Dan Smith

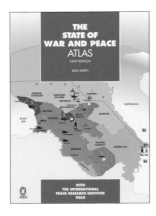

THE STATE OF WAR AND PEACE ATLAS
second edition
by Dan Smith

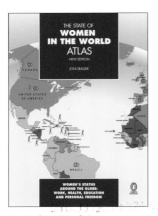

**THE STATE OF
WOMEN IN THE WORLD ATLAS**
second edition
by Joni Seager

THE STATE OF CHINA ATLAS

Robert Benewick and Stephanie Donald

PENGUIN
REFERENCE

PENGUIN REFERENCE

Published by the Penguin Group
Penguin Books Limited, 27 Wrights Lane,
London W8 5TZ, England
Penguin Putnam Inc., 375 Hudson Street,
New York, New York 10014, USA
Penguin Books Australia Limited,
Ringwood, Victoria, Australia
Penguin Books Canada Limited, 10 Alcorn Avenue,
Toronto, Ontario, Canada M4V
Penguin Books (NZ) Limited, 182-190 Wairau Road,
Auckland 10, New Zealand

Penguin Books Limited, Registered Offices:
Harmondsworth, Middlesex, England

First published in Penguin Reference 1999
10 9 8 7 6 5 4 3 2 1

Text copyright ©
Robert Benewick and Stephanie Donald, 1999
Map illustrations and graphics copyright ©
Myriad Editions Limited, 1999
All rights reserved

Penguin Reference paperback 0 14 05.1458 9

Produced for the Penguin Group by
Myriad Editions Limited
53 Old Steine, Brighton BN1 1NH, UK
myriad@dircon.co.uk

Edited and co-ordinated for Myriad Editions
by Anne Benewick and Candida Lacey
with Jannet King

Graphic design by Corinne Pearlman
Text design by Pentagram Design Limited
Maps created by Isabelle Lewis

Printed and bound in China
Produced by Phoenix Offset Limited
under the supervision of The Hanway Press, London

In memory of

Anne Benewick

P74619

CONTENTS

INTRODUCTION

China is a current friend and seen as the potential enemy. China is home. China is the Forbidden City, the Great Wall, the Terracotta Army. China is one-child-family policies. China is the abuse of human rights. China is stir-fry, dumplings, and Peking Duck. China is martial arts and opera. China is new-wave cinema and Gong Li. China is beautiful children and high-achieving students. China is pandas. China is bicycles. China is festivals and dragon-boat races. China is Hong Kong. China is Mao Zedong and Deng Xiaoping. China is business. China is Communism. The list is endless. These and many more images form most people's impression of China.

Our personal list is shorter. It is over one billion people, 22 percent of the world's population, struggling for survival and for some happiness. It is the lone person facing the tanks during the Tiananmen protest of 1989. It is many dear, generous, and loving friends. The challenge for us was how to make China comprehensible and compatible with these popular images and with our personal views. How does China translate to the scholar, student, business person, tourist, and general reader?

On October 1, 1949 Mao Zedong with his closest comrades stood on the rostrum over looking Tiananmen Square in Beijing and proclaimed the founding of the People's Republic of China. He declared that "China has stood up." On October 1, 1999 a new Chinese leadership will stand on the same rostrum on the occasion of the 50th anniversary of the People's Republic of China. They may, with every justification, claim once again that "China has stood up." There is much to celebrate but also many problems to contemplate. This atlas is our attempt to analyse China's achievements and its dilemmas on the eve of the Millenium.

Contrary to widely held beliefs, there is no shortage of data on China. The challenge is how to interpret and present them. We have relied mainly on official data, well aware of their strengths and weaknesses. We are confident of their usefulness as a guide for understanding trends, and developments, and for providing overviews. Since they are the ones in general use, we also feel that they are less confusing for the reader who may wish to consult other sources. We are less confident about specific data and advise reasonable caution. These can be distorted by their method of collection or through the manner of reporting. At the same time, China's gathering and processing techniques have become progressively more sophisticated and monitoring technologies more rigorous. There remain general problems not specific to China, however. For example, the different methodologies used to measure poverty. The Hong Kong Special Administrative Region uses its own independent statistical system and is treated comparatively where relevant.

This atlas is very much a collective undertaking ,with many people making substantial contributions. As with all Myriad atlases, Anne Benewick was the inspiration and creative genius behind it. She was actively working with us, often in great pain, until four days before she died. We would not have continued if it was not for Candida Lacey, who was the driving force towards completion. Her contribution was no less than a tour de force. Corinne Pearlman postponed other plans and travels in order to finish the atlas, such was her commitment to Anne and to Myriad. Isabelle Lewis has worked tirelessly, incorporating an additional workload and new responsibilities. In the final stages of working on the atlas, Jannet King's energy and good humor, as well as her eager eye for detail, have been vital. Laurel Johnson was an inspiring and dedicated research assistant to the project, funded by a Murdoch University grant.

We have greatly valued the continued encouragement and support of our publishers: Henry Dougier at Éditions Autrement in Paris and Hugh Rawson at Penguin Putnam in New York.

So many others have helped with their advice, sources, and support that we live in fear of accidentally missing out someone. They all loom large, including Marc Blecher, Ken Campbell at the Wogen Group, Chen Shuping, Sarah Cook, Lisa Croll, Rosemary Foot, Penny Kane, Lin Su, Judith Mackay, Murdoch University (SSHE), Laura Rivkin at the Great Britain China Center, David Simpson, the late Gordon White, Zhang Jian and The Asia Research Centre at Murdoch University.

Robert Benewick
Stephanie Donald
May 1999

Women in China are increasingly outnumbered by men. In 1999, the Chinese Academy of Social Sciences estimated that one in six men or 110 million, more than the population of Mexico, would not be able to find a wife.

Part One
DEMOGRAPHICS

YOU CANNOT WRAP A FIRE IN PAPER

One fifth of the world's population lives in China. The sheer numbers involved affect all aspects of life. The population continues to increase – even though the rates of growth have slowed. As the population clock suggests, these numbers challenge available solutions.

China's population is unevenly distributed across its provinces. Urban areas are becoming more overcrowded as the rural population flocks to cities and to the eastern region in search of work. In 1998, an estimated 120 million migrant workers left the countryside for cities.

In China, there are five times as many people as in the USA and more than twice as many as in Europe.

POPULATION CLOCK
Increase in population of China *1996*

1 056 666 7	a month
243 846	a week
34 835	a day
1 451	an hour
24	a minute

HEILONGJIANG

JILIN

LIAONING

XINJIANG

INNER MONGOLIA AR

GANSU

BEIJING

TIANJIN

HEBEI

NINGXIA AR

SHANXI

SHANDONG

QINGHAI

SHAANXI

HENAN

JIANGSU

ANHUI

SHANGHAI

TIBET

SICHUAN

HUBEI

ZHEJIANG

JIANGXI

HUNAN

GUIZHOU

FUJIAN

YUNNAN

GUANGXI AR

TAIWAN

GUANGDONG

HAINAN

POPULATION DENSITY
1995 numbers per sq k

national average: 126

▓	Eastern region 383
▓	Central region 147
░	Western region 51

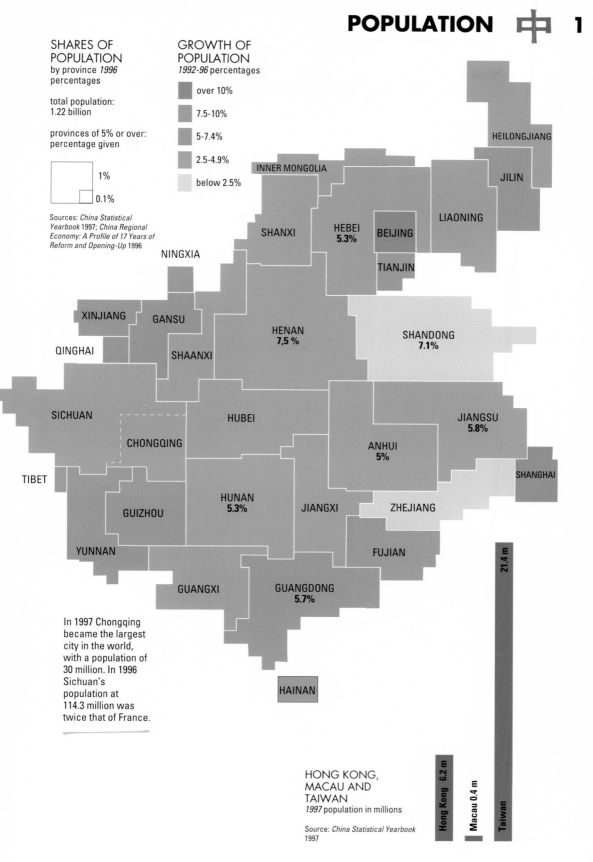
SHARES OF POPULATION
by province *1996*
percentages

total population:
1.22 billion

provinces of 5% or over:
percentage given

	1%
	0.1%

Sources: *China Statistical Yearbook* 1997; *China Regional Economy: A Profile of 17 Years of Reform and Opening-Up* 1996

GROWTH OF POPULATION
1992-96 percentages

- over 10%
- 7.5-10%
- 5-7.4%
- 2.5-4.9%
- below 2.5%

HEILONGJIANG

JILIN

INNER MONGOLIA

LIAONING

SHANXI

HEBEI
5.3%

BEIJING

NINGXIA

TIANJIN

XINJIANG

GANSU

HENAN
7,5 %

SHANDONG
7.1%

QINGHAI

SHAANXI

SICHUAN

HUBEI

JIANGSU
5.8%

CHONGQING

ANHUI
5%

SHANGHAI

TIBET

GUIZHOU

HUNAN
5.3%

JIANGXI

ZHEJIANG

YUNNAN

FUJIAN

GUANGXI

GUANGDONG
5.7%

In 1997 Chongqing became the largest city in the world, with a population of 30 million. In 1996 Sichuan's population at 114.3 million was twice that of France.

HAINAN

Hong Kong **6.2 m**

Macau **0.4 m**

Taiwan **21.4 m**

HONG KONG, MACAU AND TAIWAN
1997 population in millions

Source: *China Statistical Yearbook* 1997

Robert Benewick and Stephanie Donald *The State of China Atlas* Copyright © Myriad Editions Limited

LEAVING THE LAND NOT THE COUNTRYSIDE

Seventy percent of China's population is in the countryside. By 2025, the urban population is expected to exceed the rural population.

People have been displaced by the reintroduction of family farming or lured to the cities in search of a better living. Many rural migrants have formed the bulk of the labor force needed for the urban construction boom or for the factories in Special Economic Zones. Others enter the cities with no work or money, and no entitlement to housing and welfare facilities. In the late 1990s, Beijing and Shanghai each had three million migrant workers.

Government reformers are trying to stem the flow of migrant workers, especially those to the more developed eastern region of China. In 1997 town and village enterprises absorbed 92 million people. The planned new cities will absorb more.

rural
70%
864 millions

urban
30%
360 millions

URBAN
POPULATIONS
as a proportion of total
populations *1995*
percentages

China's population is
predominantly rural.

Source: Asian Development
Bank / UN *World
Urbanization Prospects*

95% Hong Kong

81.3% S. Korea

60.9% Mongolia

57.4% Taiwan

54.2% Philippines
53.7% Malaysia

35.4% Indonesia

30.3% China

India 26.8%

Vietnam 20.8%

China plans to build
600 new cities by the
year 2011.

MAJOR CITIES

city provinces
1997

other cities
*5 million people
or more 1996*

Source: *China Statistical
Yearbook* 1997

HEILONGJIANG

Harbin

Changchun

JILIN

LIAONING

Shenyang

INNER MONGOLIA

BEIJING Chengde

HEBEI TIANJIN Dalian

Shijazhuang

Jinan

SHANXI SHANDONG Qingdao

JIANGSU

Xi'an

SHAANXI HENAN
Zhengzhou

ANHUI Nanjing

HUBEI SHANGHAI

Wuhan Hangzhou

Chengdu Chongqing ZHEJIANG

CHONGQING JIANGXI Ningbo

Changsha

GUIZHOU HUNAN FUJIAN

YUNNAN Guangzhou Fuzhou

GUANGXI AR TAIWAN

HONG
KONG SAR

GUANGDONG

HAINAN

XINJIANG

GANSU

QINGHAI

NINGXIA
AR

TIBET

SICHUAN

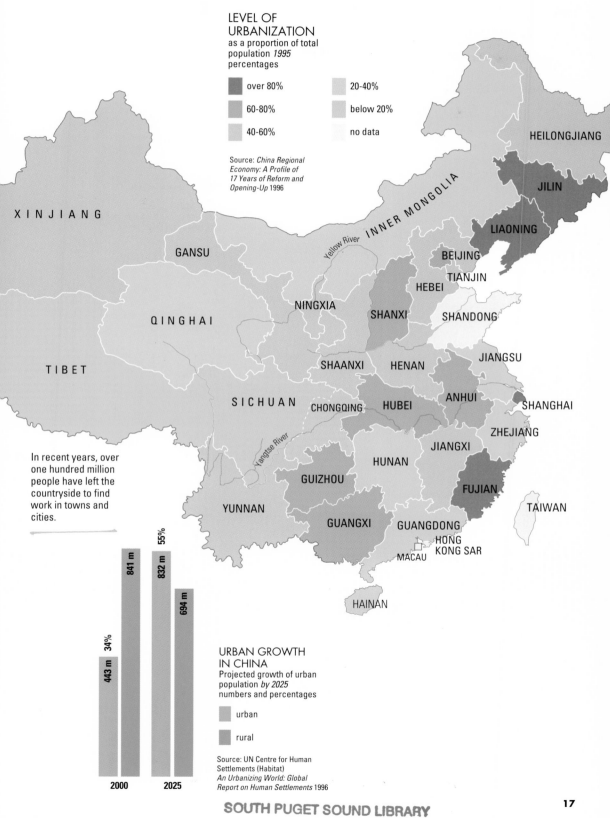

LEVEL OF
URBANIZATION
as a proportion of total
population *1995*
percentages

- over 80%
- 60-80%
- 40-60%
- 20-40%
- below 20%
- no data

Source: *China Regional
Economy: A Profile of
17 Years of Reform and
Opening-Up* 1996

XINJIANG

GANSU

INNER MONGOLIA

Yellow River

HEILONGJIANG

JILIN

LIAONING

BEIJING

TIANJIN

HEBEI

SHANXI

SHANDONG

QINGHAI

NINGXIA

TIBET

SHAANXI

HENAN

JIANGSU

SICHUAN

CHONGQING

HUBEI

ANHUI

SHANGHAI

Yangtse River

ZHEJIANG

JIANGXI

HUNAN

FUJIAN

GUIZHOU

TAIWAN

YUNNAN

GUANGXI

GUANGDONG

HONG
KONG SAR

MACAU

HAINAN

In recent years, over
one hundred million
people have left the
countryside to find
work in towns and
cities.

443 m | 34%
841 m
832 m | 55%
694 m

URBAN GROWTH
IN CHINA
Projected growth of urban
population *by 2025*
numbers and percentages

- urban
- rural

Source: UN Centre for Human
Settlements (Habitat)
*An Urbanizing World: Global
Report on Human Settlements* 1996

2000   **2025**

MAGGOTS IN THE RICE

There are more boys than girls in China. This is particularly true in the rural areas where boys are seen as more productive in agricultural work, and more valuable to aging parents. The consequences of small- or one-child family policies has been severe for girl children in the countryside. Stories of abandonment and neglect are common, and tales of abductions – of adolescent girls and young women – suggest a widening gender gap amongst under 30-year-olds.

The story is not straightforward, however. China's market-orientated economy has reduced the effectiveness of the state's ability to limit population. At the same time, it has presented incentives for individuals to voluntarily limit their fertility. Urban Chinese are rearing highly-educated girl children.

Longevity is also increasing, and women are living longer than men. This may influence China's sex ratio and begin to correct the gender imbalance.

ONE-CHILD FAMILY POLICIES

1980-95
Minority nationalities have generally been allowed more flexibility in family size.

1980
One-child family policy introduced. China aims to limit total population to 1.2 billion by 2000

1980
Marriage law bans infanticide

1984
One-child policy becomes more flexible, especially for rural Chinese whose first child was a girl

1989
Official population exceeds 1.1 billion

1991
Stricter controls introduced

1995
Incentives provided for rural households to limit family size. Official population exceeds 1.2 billion

1996
Population growth rate, is just over 1%, and continues to decline

1998
Family-planning policy to continue for another 50 years. Government aims to keep China's population below 1.6 billion by mid-21st century

Sources: Mackerras, 1997; *China Statistical Yearbook* 1997; press reports

The growing shortage of women of marriageable age has led to criminal exploitation of women. Between 1991 and 1996, Chinese police freed 88,000 kidnapped women and children and arrested 143,000 people for their part in the slave trade.

URBAN AND RURAL BIRTHS
per 100 population
1990-1996

■ urban

■ rural

Source: *China Statistical Yearbook* 1997

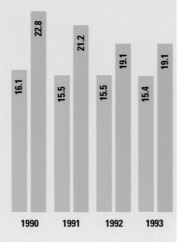

	1990	1991	1992	1993	1994	1995	1996
urban	16.1	15.5	15.5	15.4	15.1	14.8	14.5
rural	22.8	21.2	19.1	19.1	18.8	18.1	18

More than 80% of women of childbearing age used some form of contraception in 1997, but the failure rate was said to be over 25%.

CONTRACEPTION
Contraceptive methods by user *1996* percentages

Source: *China Population Statistics Yearbook* 1997

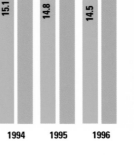

IUD	female sterilization	male sterilization	condoms	pill/injection	other
38.8%	36%	9.3%	3.5%	2.5%	1%

SEX RATIOS AT BIRTH
Number of boys born per 100 girls by province *October 1994- September 1995*

National average: 115.6

Without intervention, the sex ratio at birth would be 105 boys for every 100 girls

Source: *China Population Statistics Yearbook* 1997

- 125 or more
- 120-124
- 115-119
- 110-114
- 105-109
- below 105
- no data

The sex ratio imbalance is due to the under-reporting of female births, especially in the countryside; differential abortion, and female infanticide.

XINJIANG

HEILONGJIANG

JILIN

LIAONING

INNER MONGOLIA

GANSU

Yellow River

BEIJING

TIANJIN

HEBEI

NINGXIA

SHANDONG

QINGHAI

SHANXI

SHAANXI

HENAN

JIANGSU

TIBET

SICHUAN

CHONGQING

HUBEI

ANHUI

SHANGHAI

Yangtse River

ZHEJIANG

JIANGXI

HUNAN

GUIZHOU

FUJIAN

YUNNAN

TAIWAN

GUANGXI

GUANGDONG

HONG KONG SAR

MACAU

HAINAN

LIFE EXPECTANCY
Increase of life expectancy of men and women, *1990, 1995 and 2050* years

- men
- women

Source: UN Bureau of the Census, 1998; *China Statistical Yearbook* 1997

	1990		1995		2050	
	66.8	70.4	68	70.6	78	83.9

WHEN THE NEST IS OVERTURNED NO EGG STAYS UNBROKEN

When the Chinese Communist Party came to power in 1949, it changed one component of the characters for ethnic names: the symbol for "dog" was replaced by the symbol for "man". Despite this auspicious start, ethnic minorities have not always been comfortable within the territory of the People's Republic of China. The Tibetans and minority nationalities in Xinjiang actively work for separation from China. The Hakka are still waiting for minority nationality status.

The state policy towards minorities grants autonomy to national minority areas, such as Inner Mongolia. National minorities have some political and cultural rights but, in practice, they enjoy little power. Many are strategically located along the country's borders and these areas are rich in natural resources. Not surprisingly, all secessionist activities are banned.

The five autonomous regions of China are Guangxi, Inner Mongolia, Ningxia, Tibet, and Xinjiang. They are not specified as such on every map.

TOTAL POPULATIONS OF MAJOR NATIONAL MINORITIES *1995 populations of more than 1 million*

Source: *China Population Statistics Yearbook* 1997

Zhuang	18.7 m
Manchu	11.5 m
Miao	10.6 m
Hui	9.3 m
Uygur	8.1 m
Tujia	7.4 m
Yi	7.3 m
Tibetan	7 m
Mongolian	6.2 m
Dong	3.5 m
Yao	3.1 m
Bouyei	2.5 m
Korean	2.5 m
Bai	2 m
Li	1.6 m
Dai	1.4 m
Hani	1.4 m

National minorities occupy 64% of the total land area of China.

AUTONOMOUS REGIONS (ARs) *1997* with date established

By 1997 there were also 30 autonomous prefectures and 94 autonomous counties.

Source: Mackerras, 1997

INNER MONGOLIA AR 1947

XINJIANG-UYGUR AR 1955

NINGXIA-HUI AR 1958

TIBET AR 1965

GUANGXI-ZHUANG AR 1958

XINJIANG

GANSU
367,000

During the late 1990s, the Dalai Lama's demands for full independence were modified to "genuine self-rule".

QINGHAI
900,000

TIBET
2 m

Lhasa

There are nearly 100,000 Tibetans living in India and 20,000 in Nepal.

SICHUAN
1 m

YUNNAN
111,000

TIBETANS

Tibet Autonomous Region

other areas with Tibetan autonomous status are in Qinghai, Gansu, Sichuan and Yunnan

area claimed by Tibetan government in exile

Tibetans *1995* total population by province

Sources: Barnett, 1994; *China Population Statistics Yearbook* 1997; Mackerras, 1997; press reports

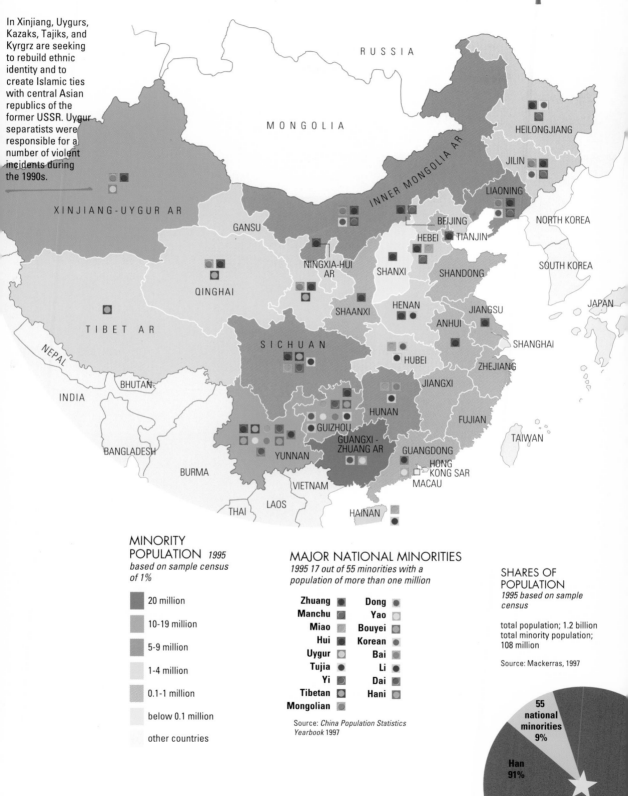

In Xinjiang, Uygurs, Kazaks, Tajiks, and Kyrgrz are seeking to rebuild ethnic identity and to create Islamic ties with central Asian republics of the former USSR. Uygur separatists were responsible for a number of violent incidents during the 1990s.

RUSSIA

MONGOLIA

HEILONGJIANG

JILIN

LIAONING

INNER MONGOLIA AR

NORTH KOREA

XINJIANG-UYGUR AR

GANSU

BEIJING

HEBEI TIANJIN

SOUTH KOREA

NINGXIA-HUI AR

SHANXI

SHANDONG

QINGHAI

SHAANXI

HENAN

JIANGSU

JAPAN

SHAANXI

ANHUI

SHANGHAI

TIBET AR

SICHUAN

HUBEI

ZHEJIANG

NEPAL

JIANGXI

BHUTAN

HUNAN

FUJIAN

INDIA

GUIZHOU

GUANGXI - ZHUANG AR

GUANGDONG

TAIWAN

BANGLADESH

YUNNAN

HONG KONG SAR

MACAU

BURMA

VIETNAM

THAI LAOS

HAINAN

MINORITY POPULATION *1995 based on sample census of 1%*

- 20 million
- 10-19 million
- 5-9 million
- 1-4 million
- 0.1-1 million
- below 0.1 million
- other countries

MAJOR NATIONAL MINORITIES
1995 17 out of 55 minorities with a population of more than one million

Zhuang		Dong	
Manchu		Yao	
Miao		Bouyei	
Hui		Korean	
Uygur		Bai	
Tujia		Li	
Yi		Dai	
Tibetan		Hani	
Mongolian			

Source: *China Population Statistics Yearbook* 1997

SHARES OF POPULATION
1995 based on sample census

total population; 1.2 billion
total minority population; 108 million

Source: Mackerras, 1997

55 national minorities 9%

Han 91%

In 1999, the National People's Congress amended the Chinese constitution, raising the status of private enterprise and opening the way for substantive guarantees of property rights.

Part Two
THE ECONOMY

Robert Benewick and Stephanie Donald *The State of China Atlas* Copyright © Myriad Editions Limited

LET SOME PEOPLE GET RICH FASTER THAN OTHERS

China's different provinces have benefited unevenly from the economic reforms that began in 1978. Despite an overall improvement in living standards, there are serious disparities between urban and rural populations, men and women, and the Eastern region and the Western hinterlands. Many people still live in poverty.

POVERTY ALLEVIATION

Regional cooperation to alleviate poverty *1996*

Source: Wong, 1998

Beijing → Inner Mongolia

Tianjin → Gansu

Shanghai → Yunnan

Guangdong → Guangxi

Jiangsu → Shaanxi

Zhejiang → Sichuan

Shandong → Xinjiang

Liaoning → Qinghai

Fujian → Ningxia

Dalian, Qingdao, Shenzhen, Ningbo → Guizhou

Western region   Eastern region   Central region

The 19 provinces and regions of central and western China are rich in natural resources but poor in infrastructure. The government has pledged to narrow the economic gap with the east by 2010.

BASIC FACILITIES

Shares of population with access to basic facilities
mid-1990s percentages

- urban
- rural

Source: Cook and White, 1997

health service: 100 / 89
safe water: 97 / 56
sanitation: 74 / 7

LIVING STANDARDS

Levels of human development based on longevity, education and income
mid-1990s

The Human Development Index provinces ranked 1 (best) to 30 (worst)

- 1-5
- 6-10
- 11-15
- 16-20
- 21-25
- 26-30

Source: *China Human Development Report* 1997

XINJIANG
GANSU
QINGHAI
TIBET
NINGXIA AR
INNER MONGOLIA AR
SHANXI
SHAANXI
HENAN
SICHUAN
CHONGQING
HUBEI
ANHUI
HEBEI
BEIJING
TIANJIN
SHANDONG
JIANGSU
SHANGHAI
ZHEJIANG
JIANGXI
HUNAN
GUIZHOU
YUNNAN
GUANGXI AR
GUANGDONG
FUJIAN
TAIWAN
HAINAN
HEILONGJIANG
JILIN
LIAONING

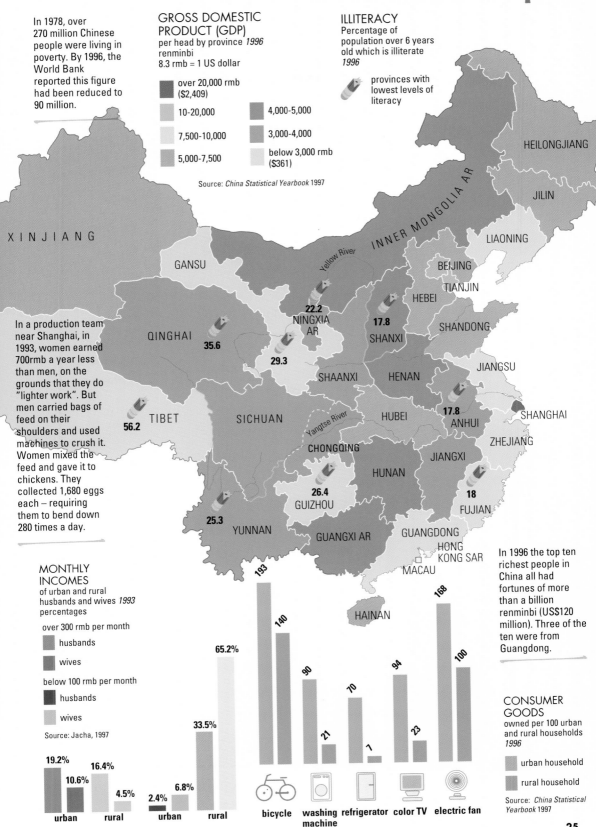

In 1978, over 270 million Chinese people were living in poverty. By 1996, the World Bank reported this figure had been reduced to 90 million.

GROSS DOMESTIC PRODUCT (GDP)
per head by province *1996*
renminbi
8.3 rmb = 1 US dollar

- over 20,000 rmb ($2,409)
- 10-20,000
- 7,500-10,000
- 5,000-7,500
- 4,000-5,000
- 3,000-4,000
- below 3,000 rmb ($361)

Source: *China Statistical Yearbook* 1997

ILLITERACY
Percentage of population over 6 years old which is illiterate *1996*

provinces with lowest levels of literacy

In a production team near Shanghai, in 1993, women earned 700rmb a year less than men, on the grounds that they do "lighter work". But men carried bags of feed on their shoulders and used machines to crush it. Women mixed the feed and gave it to chickens. They collected 1,680 eggs each – requiring them to bend down 280 times a day.

HEILONGJIANG

JILIN

XINJIANG

INNER MONGOLIA AR

LIAONING

GANSU

Yellow River

BEIJING

TIANJIN

HEBEI

22.2
NINGXIA AR

SHANXI
17.8

SHANDONG

QINGHAI
35.6

29.3

SHAANXI

HENAN

JIANGSU

56.2 TIBET

SICHUAN

Yangtse River

HUBEI

ANHUI
17.8

SHANGHAI

ZHEJIANG

CHONGQING

HUNAN

JIANGXI

26.4
GUIZHOU

18
FUJIAN

25.3
YUNNAN

GUANGXI AR

GUANGDONG

HONG KONG SAR

MACAU

HAINAN

In 1996 the top ten richest people in China all had fortunes of more than a billion renminbi (US$120 million). Three of the ten were from Guangdong.

MONTHLY INCOMES
of urban and rural husbands and wives *1993*
percentages

over 300 rmb per month
- husbands
- wives

below 100 rmb per month
- husbands
- wives

Source: Jacha, 1997

19.2%
10.6%
16.4%
4.5%

2.4%
6.8%
33.5%
65.2%

urban | rural
urban | rural

bicycle 193 140
washing machine 90 21
refrigerator 70 7
color TV 94 23
electric fan 168 100

CONSUMER GOODS
owned per 100 urban and rural households *1996*

- urban household
- rural household

Source: *China Statistical Yearbook* 1997

Robert Benewick and Stephanie Donald *The State of China Atlas* Copyright © Myriad Editions Limited

BREAKING THE IRON RICE BOWL

Economic reforms have benefited many, but at a cost to job security.

Reforming the state industries to make them pay their way could involve losing a third of the workforce.

In the countryside, the return to household farming has produced 130 million surplus workers and a huge mobile population seeking work in local industry and in the prosperous provinces of the east.

Urban unemployment is estimated officially at 3.1 percent. The true figure is much higher. Without the informal economy it would be higher still.

UNEMPLOYMENT
1996 percentages
unemployed
aged 15 and over

Source: *ILO Yearbook* 1997

- 12.4% France
- 11.3% Sri Lanka
- 8.8% Germany
- 8.6% Australia
- 8.2% UK
- 7.4% Philippines
- 5.4% USA
- 5.4% Pakistan
- 4.3% Macau
- 4% Indonesia
- 3.4% Japan
- 3% urban China
- 3% Singapore
- Hong Kong 2.8%
- 2.6% Malaysia
- Bangladesh 2.5%
- 2% South Korea

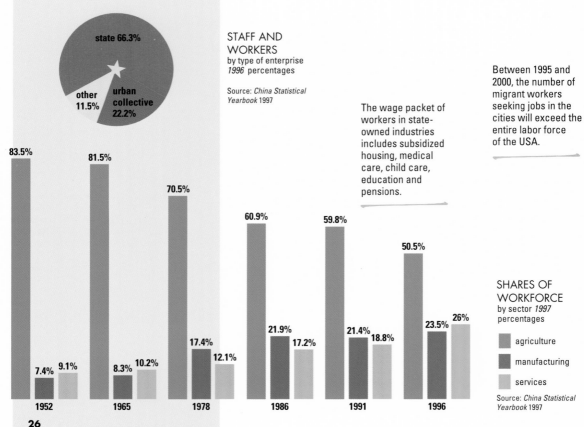

state 66.3%

other 11.5%

urban collective 22.2%

STAFF AND WORKERS
by type of enterprise
1996 percentages

Source: *China Statistical Yearbook* 1997

The wage packet of workers in state-owned industries includes subsidized housing, medical care, child care, education and pensions.

Between 1995 and 2000, the number of migrant workers seeking jobs in the cities will exceed the entire labor force of the USA.

SHARES OF WORKFORCE
by sector *1997*
percentages

- agriculture
- manufacturing
- services

Source: *China Statistical Yearbook* 1997

1952	1965	1978	1986	1991	1996
83.5%	81.5%	70.5%	60.9%	59.8%	50.5%
7.4%	8.3%	17.4%	21.9%	21.4%	23.5%
9.1%	10.2%	12.1%	17.2%	18.8%	26%

SHARES OF WORKFORCE
in total population over 15 years old *1995* percentages

- 80% and over
- 77% – 79%
- 74% – 76%
- 71% – 74%
- 70% and below
- no data

WORKFORCE BY GENDER
1995 percentages of total

- 54 men
- 46 women

workforce: 698 million, excluding Hong Kong

Source: *China Population Statistics Yearbook* 1997

Gender figures by province (men/women)

- XINJIANG — 56 / 44
- GANSU — 54 / 46
- QINGHAI — 55 / 45
- TIBET — 52 / 48
- NINGXIA AR — 53 / 47
- INNER MONGOLIA AR — 55 / 45
- HEILONGJIANG — 60 / 40
- JILIN — 58 / 42
- LIAONING — 57 / 43
- HEBEI — 54 / 46
- SHANXI — 60 / 40
- BEIJING
- TIANJIN — 57 / 43
- SHANDONG — 53 / 47
- SHAANXI — 54 / 46
- HENAN — 53 / 47
- ANHUI — 53 / 47
- JIANGSU — 51 / 49
- SHANGHAI — 54 / 46
- SICHUAN — 52 / 48
- CHONGQING
- HUBEI — 54 / 46
- ZHEJIANG — 59 / 41
- GUIZHOU — 53 / 47
- HUNAN — 55 / 45
- JIANGXI — 55 / 45
- FUJIAN — 59 / 41
- TAIWAN — 61 / 39
- YUNNAN — 53 / 47
- GUANGXI AR — 53 / 47
- GUANGDONG — 54 / 46
- HONG KONG SAR
- MACAU — 61 / 39
- HAINAN — 53 / 47

CONTRACT WORKERS IN INDUSTRY
by type of enterprise *1996* percentages

- state 73.2%
- other 8.4%
- urban collective 18.4%

Source: *China Statistical Yearbook* 1997

CONTRACT WORKERS
as a proportion of all workers 1984-96 percentages

Source: *China Labor Statistical Yearbook* 1997

- 1984 1.8%
- 1986 3.9%
- 1988 9.1%
- 1990 12.1%
- 1992 17.2%
- 1994 25.9%
- 1996 51.1%

UNEMPLOYMENT
Numbers registered unemployed and laid off *1995* urban areas

- above 600,000
- 400,000 – 600,000
- 200,000 – 400,000
- 100,000 – 200,000
- below 100,000
- not applicable

Cities marked: Shenyang, Beijing, Tianjin, Shanghai, Chongqing, Wuhan, Guangzhou

Source: *China Labor Statistical Yearbook* 1996

THE THUNDER IS HUGE BUT THE RAINDROPS ARE MANY

Farmers are leaving the land or working in subsidiary trades to subsidize their income.

Agriculture, once the ideological centerpiece of Maoist China, is a declining share of China's Gross National Product (GNP). Traditional crops are not sufficiently profitable, and farmers are growing a greater range of produce to sell to town and city markets.

Government investment is targeting agricultural modernization in an attempt to revive rural confidence and productivity.

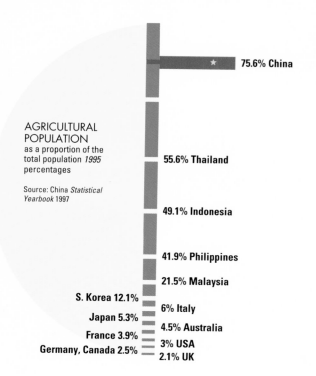

AGRICULTURAL POPULATION
as a proportion of the total population *1995* percentages

Source: China *Statistical Yearbook* 1997

75.6% China

55.6% Thailand

49.1% Indonesia

41.9% Philippines

21.5% Malaysia

S. Korea 12.1%

Japan 5.3%

France 3.9%

Germany, Canada 2.5%

6% Italy

4.5% Australia

3% USA

2.1% UK

Farmers are flooding to cities in search of work. A hundred million people are said to have left the land in 1996 alone.

In 1996, more than three quarters of the basic incomes of agricultural workers came from household business.

RURAL INCOME
Net income per person in rural households
1996 renminbi

national average:
1,926.07 renminbi (US$232)

- above 3,000 renminbi ($361)
- 2,501-3,000 renminbi ($301-$361)
- 2,001-2,500 renminbi ($241-$301)
- 1,501-2,000 renminbi ($181-$241)
- 1,500 renminbi and below ($181)

Source: *China Statistical Yearbook* 1996

HEILONGJIANG
Harbin
Changchun
JILIN
LIAONING
Chengde
Shenyang
BEIJING
Dalian
HEBEI TIANJIN
Shijiazhuang
Jinan
Qingdao
SHANDONG
Zhengzhou
HENAN
JIANGSU
ANHUI Nanjing
Hangzhou SHANGHAI
Wuhan Ningbo
HUBEI ZHEJIANG
CHONGQING
Chongqing HUNAN JIANGXI
Changsha
Fuzhou
GUIZHOU FUJIAN
YUNNAN
Guangzhou
GUANGXI AR TAIWAN
GUANGDONG
HAINAN

XINJIANG
GANSU
INNER MONGOLIA AR
QINGHAI
NINGXIA AR
SHANXI
Xi'an
SHAANXI
SICHUAN
Chengdu
TIBET

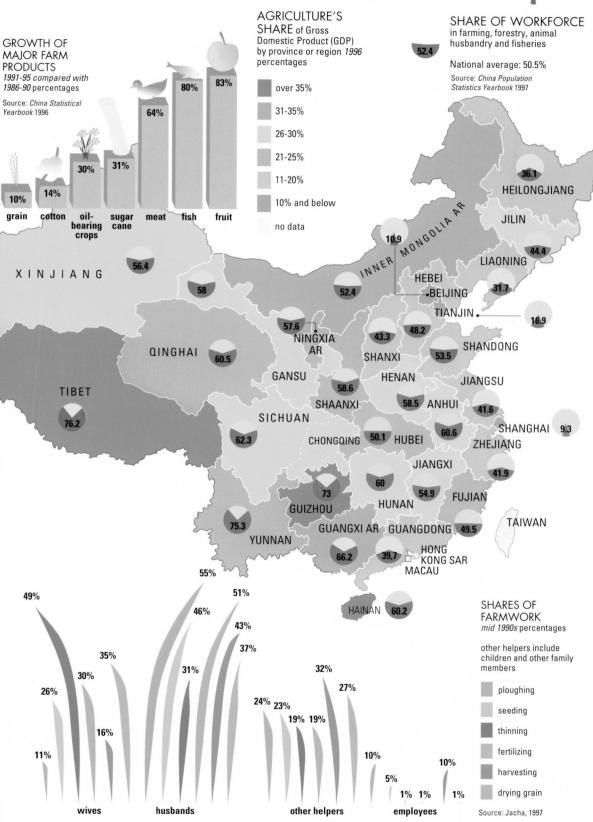

GROWTH OF MAJOR FARM PRODUCTS
1991-95 compared with 1986-90 percentages

Source: *China Statistical Yearbook* 1996

- grain 10%
- cotton 14%
- oil-bearing crops 30%
- sugar cane 31%
- meat 64%
- fish 80%
- fruit 83%

AGRICULTURE'S SHARE of Gross Domestic Product (GDP)
by province or region *1996* percentages

- over 35%
- 31-35%
- 26-30%
- 21-25%
- 11-20%
- 10% and below
- no data

SHARE OF WORKFORCE
in farming, forestry, animal husbandry and fisheries

National average: 50.5%

Source: *China Population Statistics Yearbook* 1997

52.4

XINJIANG 56.4

58

INNER MONGOLIA AR 10.9

52.4

HEILONGJIANG 36.1

JILIN

LIAONING 44.4

HEBEI

BEIJING

TIANJIN 31.7

16.9

57.6

NINGXIA AR

SHANXI 43.3

48.2

SHANDONG 53.5

QINGHAI 60.5

GANSU

HENAN 58.6

SHAANXI

JIANGSU 41.6

TIBET 76.2

SICHUAN 62.3

CHONGQING

ANHUI 58.5

HUBEI 50.1

60.6

SHANGHAI 9.3

ZHEJIANG 41.9

JIANGXI

HUNAN 60

54.9

FUJIAN 49.5

GUIZHOU 73

GUANGXI AR 66.2

GUANGDONG 39.7

HONG KONG SAR

MACAU

TAIWAN

YUNNAN 75.3

HAINAN 60.2

SHARES OF FARMWORK
mid 1990s percentages

other helpers include children and other family members

- ploughing
- seeding
- thinning
- fertilizing
- harvesting
- drying grain

Source: Jacha, 1997

wives: 49%, 26%, 30%, 35%, 16%, 11%

husbands: 55%, 51%, 46%, 43%, 37%, 31%

other helpers: 24%, 23%, 19%, 19%, 32%, 27%, 10%

employees: 5%, 1%, 1%, 10%, 1%

MANAGE THE LARGE, LET GO THE SMALL

State-owned industrial enterprises are at the top of the government's reform agenda. Most will be sold, merged, or closed down. Only 512, of 118,000 in total, will remain entirely state-owned. However, these account for nearly half of the state's assets.

SUBSIDIZED FACILITIES FOR WORKERS AND THEIR FAMILIES
provided by state owned enterprises *mid 1990s*

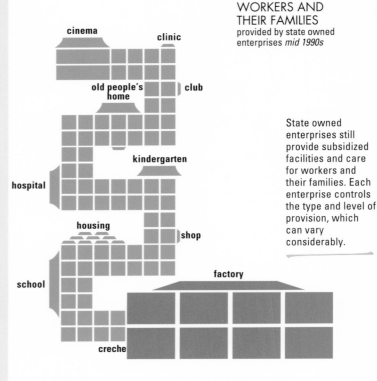

cinema
clinic
old people's home
club
kindergarten
hospital
housing
shop
school
factory
creche

State owned enterprises still provide subsidized facilities and care for workers and their families. Each enterprise controls the type and level of provision, which can vary considerably.

private, joint ventures and self-employed **24%**

town and village enterprises **35%**

state-owned enterprises **41%**

SHARES OF GDP
by type of industry *1996* percentages

Source: *Far Eastern Economic Review* 1997

SHARES OF GROSS INDUSTRIAL OUTPUT
by type of enterprise *1996* percentages

total industrial output 1996: 9960 billion renminbi (US $1200 billion)

Source: *China Statistical Yearbook* 1997

state owned enterprises **28.5%**

other type **16.6%**

collectives **39.4%**

individually owned **15.5%**

GROWTH IN NUMBERS EMPLOYED
in town and village enterprises (TVEs) millions

In 1995, only 7% of TVEs were owned by township or villages, but they employed more than 40% of the total TVE workforce.

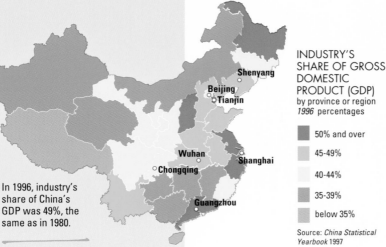

Shenyang
Beijing
Tianjin
Wuhan
Shanghai
Chongqing
Guangzhou

INDUSTRY'S SHARE OF GROSS DOMESTIC PRODUCT (GDP)
by province or region *1996* percentages

- 50% and over
- 45-49%
- 40-44%
- 35-39%
- below 35%

Source: *China Statistical Yearbook* 1997

In 1996, industry's share of China's GDP was 49%, the same as in 1980.

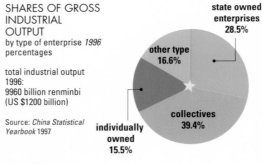

28 m	30 m	70 m	93 m	129 m	135 m
1978	1980	1985	1990	1995	1996

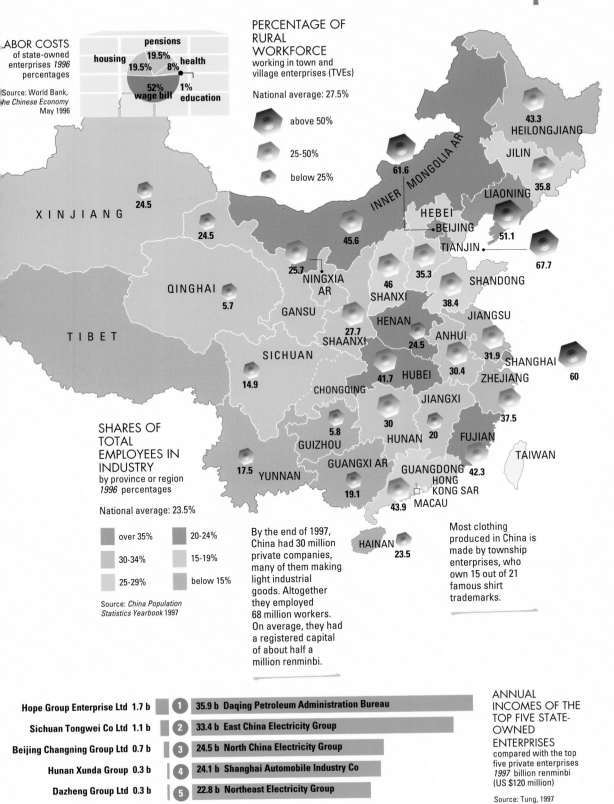

LABOR COSTS
of state-owned
enterprises *1996*
percentages

Source: World Bank,
he Chinese Economy
May 1996

pensions
19.5%
housing **8%** **health**
19.5%
52% **1%**
wage bill **education**

PERCENTAGE OF RURAL WORKFORCE
working in town and
village enterprises (TVEs)

National average: 27.5%

- above 50%
- 25-50%
- below 25%

XINJIANG 24.5

24.5

INNER MONGOLIA AR 61.6

45.6

HEILONGJIANG 43.3

JILIN 35.8

LIAONING 51.1

HEBEI
BEIJING
TIANJIN 67.7

25.7
NINGXIA AR

35.3 **SHANDONG**

QINGHAI 5.7

GANSU

46
SHANXI

38.4

JIANGSU

TIBET

27.7
SHAANXI

HENAN
24.5 **ANHUI**

31.9 **SHANGHAI** 60

SICHUAN
14.9

41.7 **HUBEI**

30.4 **ZHEJIANG**

CHONGQING

JIANGXI
37.5

5.8
GUIZHOU

30
HUNAN 20

FUJIAN 42.3

TAIWAN

17.5 **YUNNAN**

GUANGXI AR
19.1

GUANGDONG
HONG KONG SAR
MACAU
43.9

SHARES OF TOTAL EMPLOYEES IN INDUSTRY
by province or region
1996 percentages

National average: 23.5%

- over 35%
- 30-34%
- 25-29%
- 20-24%
- 15-19%
- below 15%

Source: *China Population
Statistics Yearbook* 1997

HAINAN 23.5

By the end of 1997,
China had 30 million
private companies,
many of them making
light industrial
goods. Altogether
they employed
68 million workers.
On average, they had
a registered capital
of about half a
million renminbi.

Most clothing
produced in China is
made by township
enterprises, who
own 15 out of 21
famous shirt
trademarks.

PRIVATE ENTERPRISES		STATE-OWNED ENTERPRISES	
Hope Group Enterprise Ltd	1.7 b	① 35.9 b	Daqing Petroleum Administration Bureau
Sichuan Tongwei Co Ltd	1.1 b	② 33.4 b	East China Electricity Group
Beijing Changning Group Ltd	0.7 b	③ 24.5 b	North China Electricity Group
Hunan Xunda Group	0.3 b	④ 24.1 b	Shanghai Automobile Industry Co
Dazheng Group Ltd	0.3 b	⑤ 22.8 b	Northeast Electricity Group

ANNUAL INCOMES OF THE TOP FIVE STATE-OWNED ENTERPRISES
compared with the top
five private enterprises
1997 billion renminbi
(US $120 million)

Source: Tung, 1997

IT DOESN'T MATTER WHAT COLOR THE CAT IS, SO LONG AS IT CATCHES THE MICE

China's open-door policies are producing a two-way boom in international tourism. Restaurants, shops, taxis, childcare and domestic help are also among those services that characterize the new China. However, these recent employment opportunities are not matched by better working conditions or job security.

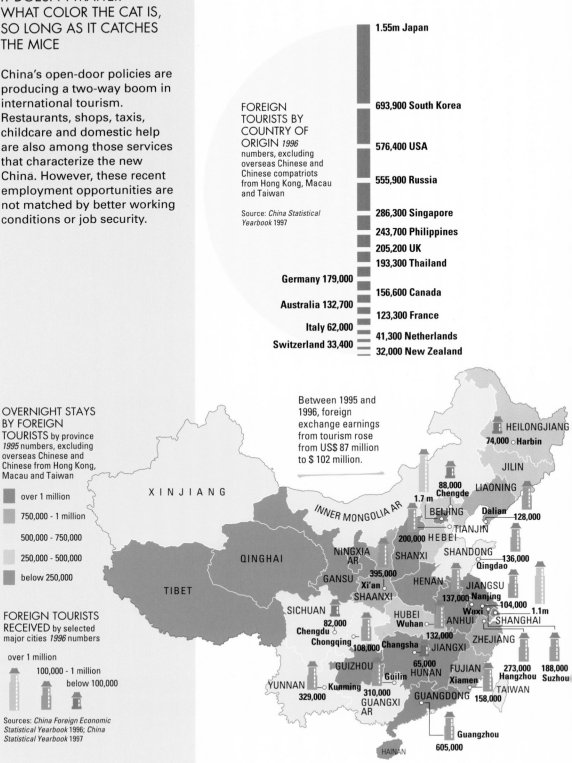

FOREIGN TOURISTS BY COUNTRY OF ORIGIN *1996*
numbers, excluding overseas Chinese and Chinese compatriots from Hong Kong, Macau and Taiwan

Source: *China Statistical Yearbook* 1997

1.55m Japan
693,900 South Korea
576,400 USA
555,900 Russia
286,300 Singapore
243,700 Philippines
205,200 UK
193,300 Thailand
Germany 179,000
156,600 Canada
Australia 132,700
123,300 France
Italy 62,000
41,300 Netherlands
Switzerland 33,400
32,000 New Zealand

OVERNIGHT STAYS BY FOREIGN TOURISTS by province *1995* numbers, excluding overseas Chinese and Chinese from Hong Kong, Macau and Taiwan

- over 1 million
- 750,000 - 1 million
- 500,000 - 750,000
- 250,000 - 500,000
- below 250,000

FOREIGN TOURISTS RECEIVED by selected major cities *1996* numbers

over 1 million
100,000 - 1 million
below 100,000

Sources: *China Foreign Economic Statistical Yearbook* 1996; *China Statistical Yearbook* 1997

Between 1995 and 1996, foreign exchange earnings from tourism rose from US$ 87 million to $ 102 million.

XINJIANG

INNER MONGOLIA AR

HEILONGJIANG
74,000 Harbin

JILIN

88,000 Chengde

1.7 m BEIJING

LIAONING

Dalian 128,000

TIANJIN

200,000 HEBEI

SHANXI

SHANDONG

136,000 Qingdao

QINGHAI

NINGXIA AR

GANSU

395,000 Xi'an

SHAANXI

HENAN

JIANGSU

137,000 Nanjing

104,000 Wuxi

1.1m SHANGHAI

TIBET

SICHUAN

82,000 Chengdu

Chongqing 108,000

HUBEI Wuhan

132,000 Changsha

ANHUI

ZHEJIANG

273,000 Hangzhou

188,000 Suzhou

JIANGXI

65,000 Guilin

HUNAN

FUJIAN Xiamen

TAIWAN

GUIZHOU

YUNNAN

329,000 Kunming

310,000 GUANGXI AR

GUANGDONG 158,000

Guangzhou 605,000

HAINAN

Service's share of China's GDP rose from 21% in 1980 to 31% in 1996.

Shanghai is being transformed into a services center for China and Asia, spelling insecurity for its large industrial workforce.

SERVICES AS SHARE OF GROSS DOMESTIC PRODUCT (GDP)
by province or region
1996 percentages

- over 40%
- 35.1-40%
- 30.1-35%
- 30% and below
- no data

SHARES OF TOTAL WORKFORCE
in services *1996*
percentages

national average: 26%

10.9

Source: *China Statistical Yearbook* 1997

INTERNATIONAL TOURIST ARRIVALS
1990 and 1996 millions and percentages

Source: *China Statistical Yearbook* 1997

Over 12% of employees in services work in the tourist industry.

By 2020, the World Tourism Organisation expects China to be the world's most popular tourist destination and the fourth largest source of international tourists.

1990
- 1.7 m (6.1%) foreign
- 0.1 m (0.3%) overseas Chinese
- 25.6 m (93.1%) Hong Kong, Macau, Taiwan

1996
- 6.7 m (13.2%) foreign
- 1.5 m (0.3%) overseas Chinese
- 44.2 m (86.5%) Hong Kong, Macau, Taiwan

Map values by province/region:
HEILONGJIANG 29.8, JILIN 29.3, INNER MONGOLIA AR 50.7, LIAONING 31.3, XINJIANG 25.6, GANSU 21.1, HEBEI 24, BEIJING, TIANJIN 35.4, SHANDONG 21.5, SHANXI 27.2, NINGXIA AR 23.3, QINGHAI 22.1, HENAN 21, SHAANXI 24.7 / 22.5, JIANGSU 25.2, ANHUI 22, SHANGHAI 41.9, ZHEJIANG 26.7, TIBET 19, SICHUAN 21.6, HUBEI 28, JIANGXI 27.2, FUJIAN 26.5, HUNAN 23.5, GUIZHOU 17.1, YUNNAN 14.8, GUANGXI AR 21.1, GUANGDONG 32.2, HONG KONG SAR, MACAU, HAINAN 28.1, TAIWAN

JOURNEY TO THE WEST: FOUR WHEELS GOOD, TWO WHEELS BAD

Bicycles in China outnumber cars by 8 to 1. Yet Western car manufacturers target China and the Chinese government encourages joint ventures with them to stimulate the economy. It is unlikely, however, that even one percent of the Chinese population will own a car in the forseeable future. Taxi companies and institutional buyers will continue to compete with bicycles to choke the roads.

INCREASE IN WATERWAY, RAIL, AND ROAD TRAVEL
1975-97 percentages

Source: *China Statistical Yearbook* 1998

11%
37%
52%

1,929 million passengers 1975

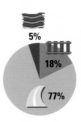

5%
18%
77%

6,202 million passengers 1985

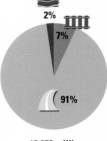

2%
7%
91%

13,253 million passengers 1997

In 1998, US automobile manufacturer General Motors announced the opening of a $1.5 billion joint venture factory with the Shanghai Automotive Corporation, marking the largest US/Chinese joint venture in China.

VEHICLE SALES IN CHINA
1992-2000 projected
1997

Source: Dolven, 1997

882,301	1,177,650	1,250,949	1,423,612	1,438,559	2,210,000
1992	1993	1994	1995	1996	2000

PUBLIC TRANSPORT IN CITIES
Number of buses and trolley buses per 10,000 people
1997

- 14 and over
- 10-13
- 6-9
- under 6

Source: *China Statistical Yearbook* 1998

A short, busy street in Beijing in 1998 became a the first to ban bicycles in favor of cars, vans, taxis, and buses.

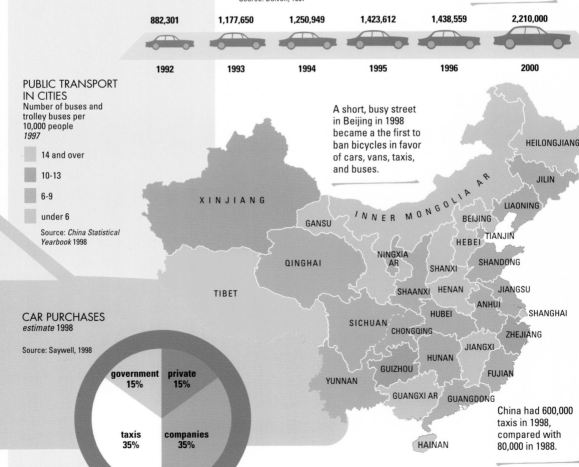

HEILONGJIANG
JILIN
XINJIANG
INNER MONGOLIA AR
LIAONING
GANSU
BEIJING
TIANJIN
HEBEI
NINGXIA AR
SHANDONG
QINGHAI
SHANXI
SHAANXI HENAN
JIANGSU
ANHUI
SHANGHAI
TIBET
HUBEI
SICHUAN
CHONGQING
ZHEJIANG
JIANGXI
HUNAN
GUIZHOU
FUJIAN
YUNNAN
GUANGXI AR GUANGDONG
HAINAN

CAR PURCHASES
estimate 1998

Source: Saywell, 1998

government 15%
private 15%
taxis 35%
companies 35%

China had 600,000 taxis in 1998, compared with 80,000 in 1988.

TRAFFIC ACCIDENTS
1997

- 20,000 and over
- 15,000-19,000
- 10,000-14,999
- 5,000-9,999
- under 5,000

Source: *China Statistical Yearbook* 1998

Two-thirds of China's traffic accidents are in the countryside.

HEILONGJIANG

JILIN

XINJIANG

INNER MONGOLIA AR

GANSU

QINGHAI

NINGXIA AR

TIBET

SHAANXI

SICHUAN

CHONGQING

GUIZHOU

YUNNAN

GUANGXI AR

HEILONGJIANG **6**

JILIN **6**

LIAONING **8**

BEIJING **14**

HEBEI TIANJIN **17**

SHANXI **12**

SHANDONG **20**

21

HENAN **8**

JIANGSU **5**

SHANGHAI **17** — **24**

ANHUI **6**

ZHEJIANG **11**

HUBEI **6**

JIANGXI **10**

HUNAN **6**

FUJIAN **24**

GUANGDONG **32**

HONG KONG SAR
MACAU

TAIWAN

XINJIANG **12**

INNER MONGOLIA AR **14**

8

4 SHAANXI **6**

QINGHAI **6**

TIBET **0.1**

SICHUAN **6**

CHONGQING **0.4**

GUIZHOU **5**

YUNNAN **6**

GUANGXI AR **14**

HAINAN **24**

BICYCLES
Number owned per 100 households *1997*

- 200 and over
- 150-199
- 100-149
- under 100
- no data

number of motorcycles per 100 households *number given*

Source: *China Statistical Yearbook* 1998

AIRPLANES
Number of civil aircraft *1985-97*

Source: *China Statistical Yearbook* 1998

421
1985

661
1990

720
1995

770
1997

A HEAVY WEIGHT HANGS BY A HAIR

China is the world's leading coal producer. Coal supplies nearly three-quarters of China's energy needs. The abundance of coal, much of it low-grade, has environmental and health costs.

Despite China's progress in energy production there are still power shortages to meet the demands of a rapidly expanding economy. Oil and gas are under-developed and hydro-power is under-used. The impact of nuclear power remains some years away, and the means of energy distribution and delivery is inadequate.

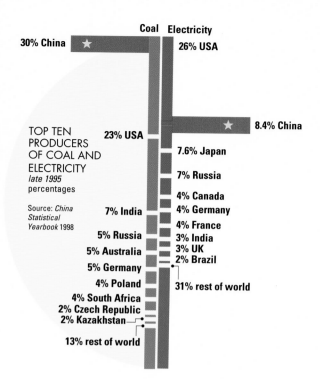

Coal **Electricity**

30% China

26% USA

8.4% China

TOP TEN PRODUCERS OF COAL AND ELECTRICITY
late 1995
percentages

Source: *China Statistical Yearbook* 1998

23% USA

7.6% Japan

7% Russia

4% Canada

4% Germany

7% India

4% France

5% Russia

3% India

5% Australia

3% UK

5% Germany

2% Brazil

4% Poland

31% rest of world

4% South Africa

2% Czech Republic

2% Kazakhstan

13% rest of world

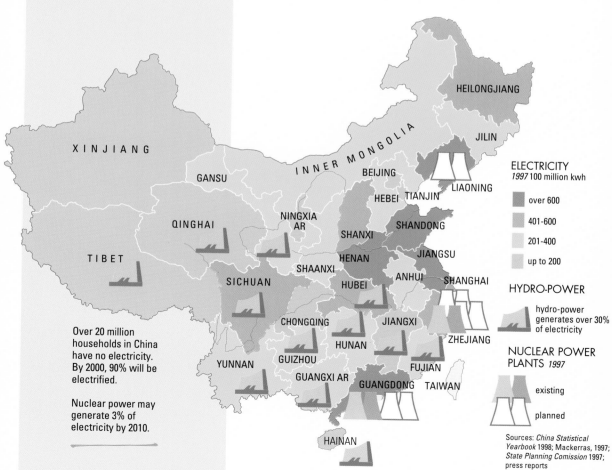

HEILONGJIANG

JILIN

XINJIANG

GANSU

INNER MONGOLIA

BEIJING

LIAONING

HEBEI TIANJIN

QINGHAI

NINGXIA AR

SHANXI

SHANDONG

TIBET

SHAANXI

HENAN

JIANGSU

SICHUAN

HUBEI

ANHUI

SHANGHAI

CHONGQING

JIANGXI

ZHEJIANG

HUNAN

YUNNAN

GUIZHOU

FUJIAN

GUANGXI AR

GUANGDONG

TAIWAN

HAINAN

ELECTRICITY
1997 100 million kwh

over 600

401-600

201-400

up to 200

HYDRO-POWER

hydro-power generates over 30% of electricity

NUCLEAR POWER PLANTS *1997*

existing

planned

Over 20 million households in China have no electricity. By 2000, 90% will be electrified.

Nuclear power may generate 3% of electricity by 2010.

Sources: *China Statistical Yearbook* 1998; Mackerras, 1997; *State Planning Comission* 1997; press reports

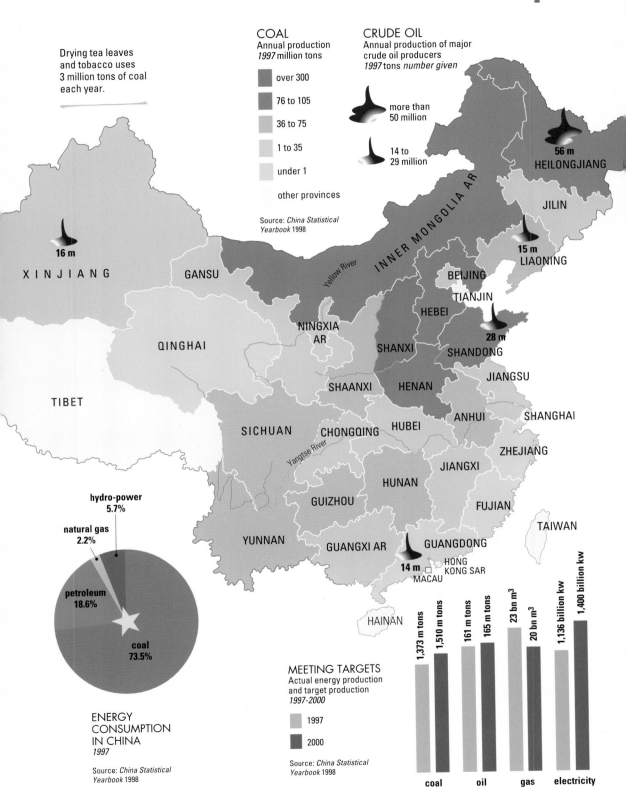

Drying tea leaves
and tobacco uses
3 million tons of coal
each year.

COAL
Annual production
1997 million tons

- over 300
- 76 to 105
- 36 to 75
- 1 to 35
- under 1
- other provinces

Source: *China Statistical Yearbook* 1998

CRUDE OIL
Annual production of major
crude oil producers
1997 tons *number given*

- more than 50 million
- 14 to 29 million

XINJIANG 16 m

GANSU

HEILONGJIANG 56 m

JILIN

LIAONING 15 m

INNER MONGOLIA AR

Yellow River

BEIJING
TIANJIN

QINGHAI

NINGXIA AR

HEBEI

SHANXI

SHANDONG 28 m

SHAANXI

HENAN

JIANGSU

TIBET

SICHUAN

CHONGQING

HUBEI

ANHUI

SHANGHAI

Yangtse River

ZHEJIANG

JIANGXI

HUNAN

FUJIAN

GUIZHOU

YUNNAN

GUANGXI AR

GUANGDONG 14 m

HONG KONG SAR
MACAU

TAIWAN

HAINAN

ENERGY CONSUMPTION IN CHINA
1997

- hydro-power 5.7%
- natural gas 2.2%
- petroleum 18.6%
- coal 73.5%

Source: *China Statistical Yearbook* 1998

MEETING TARGETS
Actual energy production
and target production
1997-2000

- 1997
- 2000

Source: *China Statistical Yearbook* 1998

coal	oil	gas	electricity
1,373 m tons / 1,510 m tons	161 m tons / 165 m tons	23 bn m³ / 20 bn m³	1,136 billion kw / 1,400 billion kw

Robert Benewick and Stephanie Donald *The State of China Atlas* Copyright © Myriad Editions Limited

JUMPING INTO THE SEA

In the mid-1990s, China was the second largest recipient after the USA of foreign direct investment.

China offered a huge domestic market, plentiful cheap labor, few restrictions on working conditions, an authoritarian government committed to advancing market reforms, and favorable investment terms. In the late 1990s, enthusiasm was dampened by the bureaucratic frustrations, the realities of the banking system, and the Asia financial crisis. Yet the inflow of investment remains impressive. Ironically the economic slowdown that has occurred is stimulating much-needed state investment in China's infrastructure.

One of the costs of the foreign direct investment boom has been its distribution. The eastern seaboard provinces, and Guangdong in particular, have benefitted disproportionately.

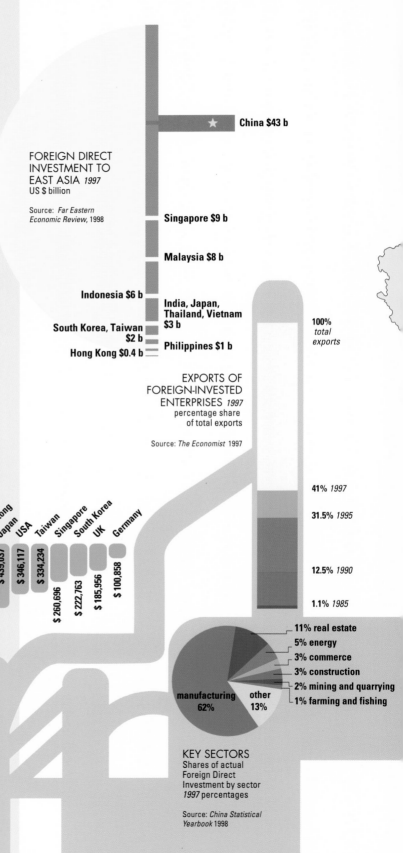

FOREIGN DIRECT INVESTMENT TO EAST ASIA *1997*
US $ billion

Source: *Far Eastern Economic Review,* 1998

China $43 b

Singapore $9 b

Malaysia $8 b

Indonesia $6 b

India, Japan, Thailand, Vietnam $3 b

South Korea, Taiwan $2 b

Philippines $1 b

Hong Kong $0.4 b

EXPORTS OF FOREIGN-INVESTED ENTERPRISES *1997*
percentage share of total exports

Source: *The Economist* 1997

100% *total exports*

41% *1997*

31.5% *1995*

12.5% *1990*

1.1% *1985*

Hong Kong $2,155,111
Japan $439,037
USA $346,117
Taiwan $334,234
Singapore $260,696
South Korea $222,763
UK $185,956
Germany $100,858

TOP INVESTORS IN CHINA *1997*
US $10,000

Source: *China Statistical Yearbook* 1998

11% real estate
5% energy
3% commerce
3% construction
2% mining and quarrying
1% farming and fishing

manufacturing 62%

other 13%

KEY SECTORS
Shares of actual Foreign Direct Investment by sector 1997 percentages

Source: *China Statistical Yearbook* 1998

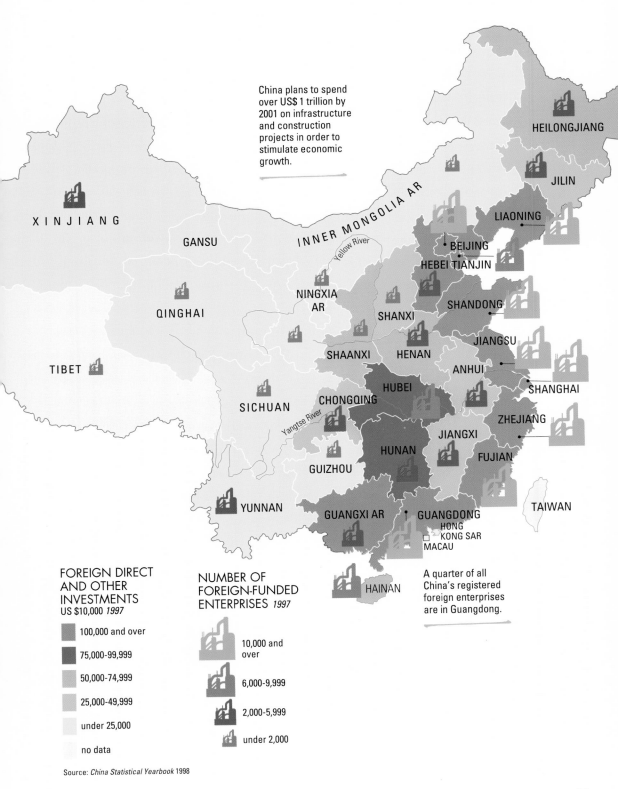

China plans to spend over US$ 1 trillion by 2001 on infrastructure and construction projects in order to stimulate economic growth.

HEILONGJIANG

JILIN

LIAONING

XINJIANG

GANSU

INNER MONGOLIA AR

Yellow River

BEIJING

HEBEI TIANJIN

SHANDONG

NINGXIA AR

SHANXI

QINGHAI

JIANGSU

SHAANXI

HENAN

ANHUI

TIBET

CHONGQING

HUBEI

SHANGHAI

SICHUAN

Yangtse River

ZHEJIANG

JIANGXI

FUJIAN

HUNAN

GUIZHOU

TAIWAN

YUNNAN

GUANGXI AR

GUANGDONG

HONG
KONG SAR
MACAU

HAINAN

A quarter of all China's registered foreign enterprises are in Guangdong.

FOREIGN DIRECT AND OTHER INVESTMENTS
US $10,000 *1997*

- 100,000 and over
- 75,000-99,999
- 50,000-74,999
- 25,000-49,999
- under 25,000
- no data

NUMBER OF FOREIGN-FUNDED ENTERPRISES *1997*

- 10,000 and over
- 6,000-9,999
- 2,000-5,999
- under 2,000

Source: *China Statistical Yearbook* 1998

WHEN AN ARROW IS ON A STRING IT MUST GO

In 1990, China was the 15th largest trading nation in the world. By 1994 it was 11th. By 1997, China including Hong Kong, was fourth.

Trade is vital to China's economic liberalization and modernization. China's success as one of the world's largest trading nations is all the more remarkable for having been achieved since 1978. During the same period, the economic gap has widened between the prosperous, booming eastern coastal provinces, Guangdong in particular, and the less-developed central and western regions. The Hong Kong Special Administrative Region, although listed separately in world trade statistics, enhances China's international economic power.

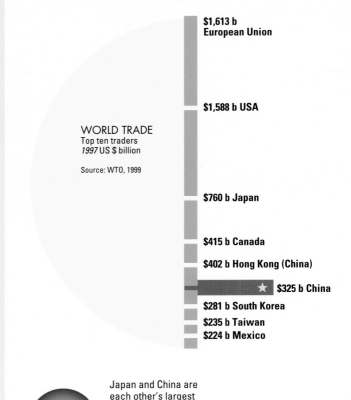

WORLD TRADE
Top ten traders
1997 US $ billion

Source: WTO, 1999

$1,613 b
European Union

$1,588 b USA

$760 b Japan

$415 b Canada

$402 b Hong Kong (China)

★ $325 b China

$281 b South Korea

$235 b Taiwan

$224 b Mexico

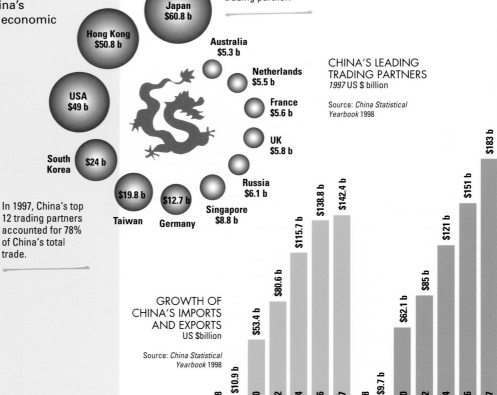

Japan and China are each other's largest trading partner.

CHINA'S LEADING TRADING PARTNERS
1997 US $ billion

Source: *China Statistical Yearbook* 1998

Japan $60.8 b

Hong Kong $50.8 b

Australia $5.3 b

Netherlands $5.5 b

France $5.6 b

USA $49 b

UK $5.8 b

South Korea $24 b

Russia $6.1 b

Taiwan $19.8 b

Germany $12.7 b

Singapore $8.8 b

In 1997, China's top 12 trading partners accounted for 78% of China's total trade.

GROWTH OF CHINA'S IMPORTS AND EXPORTS
US $billion

Source: *China Statistical Yearbook* 1998

Imports

1978	1990	1992	1994	1996	1997
$10.9 b	$53.4 b	$80.6 b	$115.7 b	$138.8 b	$142.4 b

Exports

1978	1990	1992	1994	1996	1997
$9.7 b	$62.1 b	$85 b	$121 b	$151 b	$183 b

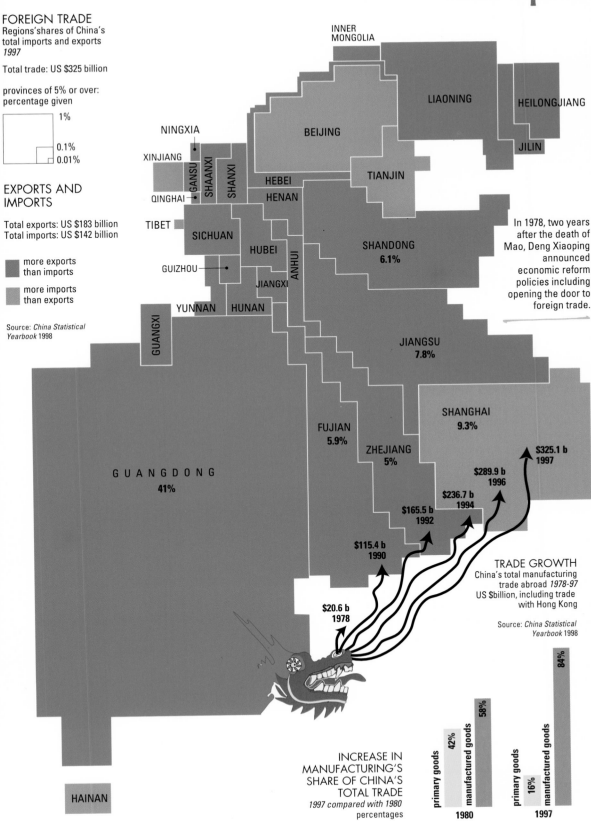

FOREIGN TRADE

Regions' shares of China's total imports and exports
1997

Total trade: US $325 billion

provinces of 5% or over:
percentage given

1%
0.1%
0.01%

EXPORTS AND IMPORTS

Total exports: US $183 billion
Total imports: US $142 billion

more exports than imports

more imports than exports

Source: *China Statistical Yearbook* 1998

In 1978, two years after the death of Mao, Deng Xiaoping announced economic reform policies including opening the door to foreign trade.

INNER MONGOLIA

LIAONING

HEILONGJIANG

NINGXIA

XINJIANG

BEIJING

GANSU

SHAANXI

SHANXI

QINGHAI

HEBEI

TIANJIN

JILIN

TIBET

HENAN

SICHUAN

HUBEI

ANHUI

SHANDONG
6.1%

GUIZHOU

JIANGXI

YUNNAN

HUNAN

GUANGXI

JIANGSU
7.8%

SHANGHAI
9.3%

FUJIAN
5.9%

ZHEJIANG
5%

GUANGDONG
41%

$325.1 b
1997

$289.9 b
1996

$236.7 b
1994

$165.5 b
1992

$115.4 b
1990

$20.6 b
1978

TRADE GROWTH

China's total manufacturing trade abroad *1978-97*
US $billion, including trade with Hong Kong

Source: *China Statistical Yearbook* 1998

HAINAN

INCREASE IN MANUFACTURING'S SHARE OF CHINA'S TOTAL TRADE

1997 compared with 1980 percentages

primary goods **42%**
manufactured goods **58%**
1980

primary goods **16%**
manufactured goods **84%**
1997

BETTER THE HEAD OF A CHICKEN THAN THE TAIL OF AN OX

Greater China is a much contested term. For some it includes all areas of the world inhabited by Chinese populations. The map below locates ethnic Chinese communities around the world. In Southeast Asia, especially, the economic power of these communities of overseas Chinese is disproportionate to their numbers.

For others, "Greater China" is confined to mainland China and to those parts of Southeast Asia which have large Chinese populations but are not subject to Chinese rule. Two of these, Hong Kong and Macau, returned to China as Special Administrative Regions (SARs) in 1997 and 1999, respectively. The third, Taiwan, is a democratic republic in dispute with China over the issue of sovereignty. All three are important sources of trade and investment for China.

Robert Benewick and Stephanie Donald *The State of China Atlas* Copyright © Myriad Editions Limited

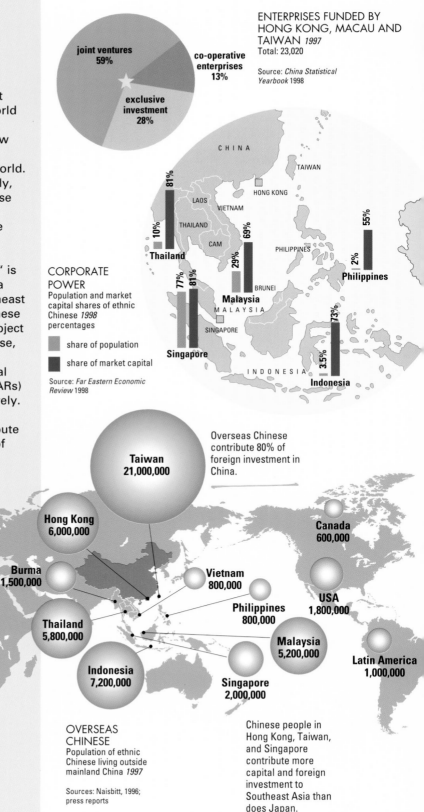

ENTERPRISES FUNDED BY HONG KONG, MACAU AND TAIWAN *1997*
Total: 23,020

Source: *China Statistical Yearbook* 1998

joint ventures 59%
co-operative enterprises 13%
exclusive investment 28%

CORPORATE POWER
Population and market capital shares of ethnic Chinese *1998* percentages

share of population
share of market capital

Source: *Far Eastern Economic Review* 1998

Thailand 10% / 81%
Malaysia 29% / 69%
Philippines 2% / 55%
Singapore 77% / 81%
Indonesia 3.5% / 73%

Overseas Chinese contribute 80% of foreign investment in China.

Taiwan 21,000,000
Hong Kong 6,000,000
Europe 600,000
Burma 1,500,000
Africa 100,000
Thailand 5,800,000
Indonesia 7,200,000
Vietnam 800,000
Philippines 800,000
Singapore 2,000,000
Malaysia 5,200,000
Canada 600,000
USA 1,800,000
Latin America 1,000,000

OVERSEAS CHINESE
Population of ethnic Chinese living outside mainland China *1997*

Sources: Naisbitt, 1996; press reports

Chinese people in Hong Kong, Taiwan, and Singapore contribute more capital and foreign investment to Southeast Asia than does Japan.

FUNDING BY ENTREPRENEURS FROM HONG KONG, MACAU AND TAIWAN
1997 100 million yuan

Assets
- over 3,000
- 500-1,000
- 100-500
- 10-100
- under 10
- no data

Investment
- over 100
- 50-100
- 10-50

Source: *China Statistical Yearbook* 1998

XINJIANG

GANSU

INNER MONGOLIA AR

HEILONGJIANG

JILIN

LIAONING

BEIJING

TIANJIN

HEBEI

SHANDONG

NINGXIA AR

QINGHAI

SHANXI

SHAANXI

HENAN

JIANGSU

SHANGHAI

TIBET

SICHUAN

CHONGQING

HUBEI

ANHUI

ZHEJIANG

JIANGXI

HUNAN

GUIZHOU

FUJIAN

TAIWAN

YUNNAN

GUANGXI AR

GUANGDONG

HONG KONG SAR

MACAU

REAL ESTATE DEVELOPMENT
Number of development companies funded by entrepreneurs from Hong Kong, Macau and Taiwan *1997*

- over 200
- 100-200
- 50-100
- under 50
- no data

Source: *China Statistical Yearbook* 1998

HEILONGJIANG

XINJIANG

GANSU

INNER MONGOLIA AR

JILIN

LIAONING

BEIJING

TIANJIN

HEBEI

HAINAN

NINGXIA AR

QINGHAI

SHANXI

SHANDONG

SHAANXI

HENAN

JIANGSU

TIBET

SICHUAN

CHONGQING

HUBEI

ANHUI

SHANGHAI

JIANGXI

ZHEJIANG

HUNAN

GUIZHOU

FUJIAN

TAIWAN

YUNNAN

GUANGXI AR

GUANGDONG

HONG KONG SAR

MACAU

HAINAN

In 1997, there were 10,000 Taiwanese companies in the coastal region of Guangdong alone.

GROSS DOMESTIC PRODUCT (GDP)
per person *1999* US dollars

Source: *Far Eastern Economic Review* 1999

China $2,800

Hong Kong $26,500

Taiwan $14,700

Reasons for joining the Chinese Communist Party:

"This is an outstanding Party with an outstanding purpose, to change society for the better. It's attractive to anyone who is searching for higher ideals in life." – Beijing University student, aged 20

"People my age joined the Party for ideals. Now, most of them are joining because they want power and seek personal gain." – veteran Party member, aged 60

THE PARTY STATE

A TIGER WHOSE BUTTOCKS MAY NOT BE TOUCHED

The Chinese Communist Party, with a membership of more than 58 million, is the largest political party in the world. This has less to do with ideological commitment than with the power it exercises and the career opportunities it offers.

The eight small democratic parties do not provide an opposition to the Communist Party. In contrast, following the Tiananmen protest of 1989, their consultative role has expanded. The founding of the China Democratic Party in 1998, following what was interpreted by observers as a "Beijing Spring" of liberalization, resulted in the imprisonment of the organizers for "subverting state power." Any challenge to the Communist Party's monopoly of power is likely to come from within its own ranks rather than from without.

INCREASE OF PARTY MEMBERSHIP
between 1st and 15th National Party Congresses
held up to 1997, numbers

Source: Zheng, 1997

Year	Congress	Members
1921	1st	57
1922	2nd	195
1923	3rd	420
1925	4th	3,000
1927	5th	57,900
1928	6th	40,000
1945	7th	1.2m
1956	8th	10.7 m
1969	9th	22 m
1973	10th	28 m
1977	11th	35 m
1982	12th	39 m
1987	13th	46 m
1992	14th	52 m
1997	15th	5

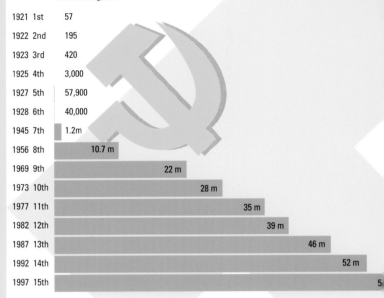

DEMOCRATIC PARTIES *1990s*
under the leadership of the Communist Party of China

Source: Mackerras, 1997

China Democratic League
September 3rd Study Society
high level academics in social and natural sciences

Chinese Peasants' and Workers' Democratic Party
China Association for Promoting Democracy
professionals, doctors

China Democratic National Construction Association
business people

Revolutionary Committee of the Guomindang
Taiwan Democratic Self-Government League
Party for Public Interest
people with Taiwan connections and overseas Chinese

INFORMAL POWER
Guanxi: using contacts, friends and family to get things done

Jiang Zemin
General Secretary of Communist Party 1989-
Chair of Central Military Commission 1989-
President of People's Republic of China 1993-

born 1926, Jiangsu, • electrical engineer • Shanghai
Jiaotong University • joined CCP 1946
• mayor of Shanghai 1985-87
• entered Politburo 1987

POWER STRUCTURE
Standing Committee of the
Politburo
seven members *1999*

Source: Nakai, 1998

Li Peng
no. 2 on Standing Committee
Chair of Standing Committee of National People's Congress

born 1928, Sichuan • hydro-electric engineer, Moscow Power
Institute • joined CCP 1945 • Premier of People's Republic of China
1987-1998, including 1989 Tiananmen Protest standing down after two
terms • entered Politburo 1985

Zhu Rongji
Premier 1998-

born 1928, Hunan • electrical engineer, Qinghua
university • joined CCP 1949 • mayor of Shanghai
1988-91 • Governor of Bank of China 1993-95 • Vice
Premier 1993-98 • entered Politburo 1992

Hu Jintao
member of Central
Secretariat, 1998-
Vice President of People's
Republic of China 1998-,
President of
Central Party School 1993-

born 1942, Anhui • hydro-
electrical engineer, Qinghua
university • joined CCP 1964 •
President, All-China Youth
Federation 1982 • party secretary,
Guizhou 1985-88 and Tibet
1988-92 • entered Politburo 1992

Li Ruihuan
Chair of Chinese People's
Political Consultative
Congress 1993-

born 1934, Tianjin • engineer,
Beijing Sparetime Architecture
Engineering Institute • during
cultural revolution: persecuted
1966-71 • joined CCP 1959 • mayor
of Tianjin 1982-89 • entered
Politburo 1987

Li Lanqing
Vice premier of
State Council 1993-

born 1932, Jiangsu • joined CCP
1952 • business management,
Fudan university, Shanghai •
Ministry of Foreign Economic
Relations and Trade 1986-93 •
entered Politburo 1992

Wei Jianxiang
Secretary of Central
Discipline Inspection
Commission 1992-,
President of
All-China Federation of Trade
Unions 1993-,
Secretary of Beijing Party
Committee 1995-,

born 1931, Zhejiang • joined CCP
1949 • engineer, Dalian
Engineering Institute •
entered Politburo 1992

Politburo
plus 15 other members (all at same level)

Central Military Commission
Chair: Jiang Zemin
Deputies
General Staff: military affairs
General Political Department:
ideology, personnel, legal
General Logistics Department: finance

Central Discipline Inspection Commission
Secretary: Wei Jianxiang

Central Committee
193 members, made up of:
151 alternate members, made up of:

local party/government officials 78		40%
central party/government officials 62		32%
PLA 42	22%	
others 11	6%	

National
Party Congress
meets every five
years
15th Congress 2048
delegates

56.3%	85	local party/government officials
11.2%	17	central party/government officials
15.3%	23	PLA
9.2%	14	economic/ enterprises
8%	12	others

TO FIND A NEEDLE OR A PEARL IN THE BIG OCEAN

China's constitution states that the National People's Congress is the highest organ of state power. Relative to the Communist Party, the State Council, and informal politics, this is not the case. The pyramids represent a more realistic hierarchy.

From 1978, however, the National People's Congress has been behaving more like a legislature familiar to Western eyes. It no longer simply rubber-stamps decisions taken elsewhere, and it has become a more professional organization with a support staff of over 3,000.

Political reform still lags behind economic reform. However, at the grass roots level, where there has been a significant growth of local industry, village committees have acquired decision-making power.

9TH NATIONAL PEOPLE'S CONGRESS
March 1998
percentages

previous
Delegates
26%

new
Delegates
74%

women
22%

men
78%

81%	9th NPC
69%	8th NPC

UNDERGRADUATE EDUCATION

AVERAGE AGE OF
2,979 NPC DELEGATES
9th NPC   52.27 years
8th NPC   53.13 years

new delegations:
Chongqing Municipality: 58 Delegates
Hong Kong SAR: 35 Delegates

33%   cadres
22%   intellectuals
19%   workers and peasants
15%   democratic parties
14%   minority nationalities
        (1 each of 55 plus Han)
9%   PLA

SHARES OF 2979 DELEGATES

LEGISLATURE

Li Peng
Chair of Standing
Committee of National
People's Congress (NPC)
also on Standing Committee of
Politburo

19 Vice Chairs

Standing Committee of NPC
155 members
Meets between NPC annual sessions

HONG KONG
Special
Administrative Region
(SAR)

Tung Chee-hwa
Chief Executive
recommended locally, appointed by
Beijing central government 1996

Legislative Council
1998 for five years
60 members

20 elected by proportional representation
30 appointed by professional and business bodies
10 appointed by 800-member election committee

**NATIONAL
PEOPLE'S
CONGRESS (NPC)**

Meets once a year
for 15 days
9th NPC (March 1998)
2979 Delegates

Nine Committees:
Nationalities Committee;
Law Committee; Internal and Judicial Affairs
Committee; Financial and Economic Committee;
Education, Science, Culture and Public Health Committee;
Foreign Affairs Committee; Overseas Chinese Committee;
Environment and Resources Protection Committee;
Agriculture and Rural Affairs Committee

FORMAL POWER STRUCTURE OF CENTRAL GOVERNMENT
1999

Source: press reports

EXECUTIVE

Jiang Zemin
President
also General Secretary of
Communist Party

Hu Jintao
Vice President
also on Standing Committee of Politburo

Zhu Rongji
Premier of
the State Council
also on Standing Committee of Politburo

Standing Committee of State Council
Premier
4 Vice Premiers
5 State Councillors
Secretary General
29 members at ministerial level

State Council
29 ministries and commissions, 51 offices, bureaux and institutions

MILITARY

Central Military
Commission (State)

Chair
Jiang Zemin
also Chair of Communist Party
Central Military Commission

JUDICIARY
Supreme
People's Court
President
Xiao Yang
Procurator General
Han Zhubin

Supreme People's
Procuratorate

**CHINESE
PEOPLE'S
POLITICAL
CONSULTATIVE
CONGRESS (CPPCC)**

Li Ruihuan
Chair, CPPCC
also on Standing Committee of
Politburo

Standing Committee of CPPCC
Chair, 31 Vice Chairs, Secretary General

The CPPCC meets once a year, in conjunction with NPC

Delegates include intellectuals, academics, business people,
technical experts, overseas Chinese, professionals, democratic
parties

SHARPENING THE WEAPONS AND FEEDING THE HORSES

The People's Liberation Army (PLA) is the largest land force in the world. Recent emphasis has been on modernization and professionalization. In 1998, in an attempt to restore the PLA's legitimacy following its role in crushing the 1989 Tiananmen protest, over a quarter of a million soldiers were mobilized to fight serious flooding. They worked beneath posters urging them to emulate the mythical Emperor Wu who supposedly tamed floods 4,000 years ago.

Equally dramatic was the order from Party-state rulers that the PLA should scale down its manufacturing for civilian purposes and its entrepreneurial activities, some of which are listed here.

A crackdown on the PLA's smuggling activities is another serious threat its power.

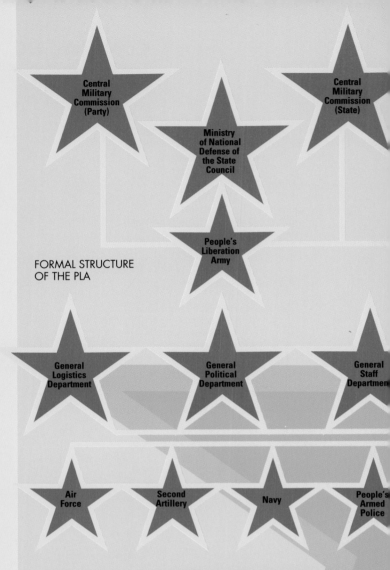

FORMAL STRUCTURE OF THE PLA

Only in wartime or during national crises would the PLA take command. Its performance in the Tiananmen protest of 1989 led to a major shake-up in the People's Armed Police (PAP) leadership and an increase in troop numbers.

COMMUNIST PARTY POLITBURO *1998*
Of the 22 members, only two are from the PLA:

Chi Haotian
State Councillor and Minister of Defense 1992-
Vice Chair of Central Military Commission 1995-
member of Central Committee since 12th Party Congress
born 1929, Shandong
joined PLA 1945
joined CCP 1946
educated in PLA's Military Academy
entered Central Military Commission 1987
promoted to General 1988
Chief of Staff 1987-92
entered Politburo 1997

Zhang Wannian
Vice Chair of Central Military Commission
in daily control of China's armed forces
member of Central Committee since 14th and 15th
Party Congresses
born 1928, Shandong
joined PLA 1944
joined CCP 1945
educated Nanjing Military Academy
Chief of PLA General Staff 1992-95
entered Central Military Commission 1992
promoted to General 1993
entered Politburo 1997

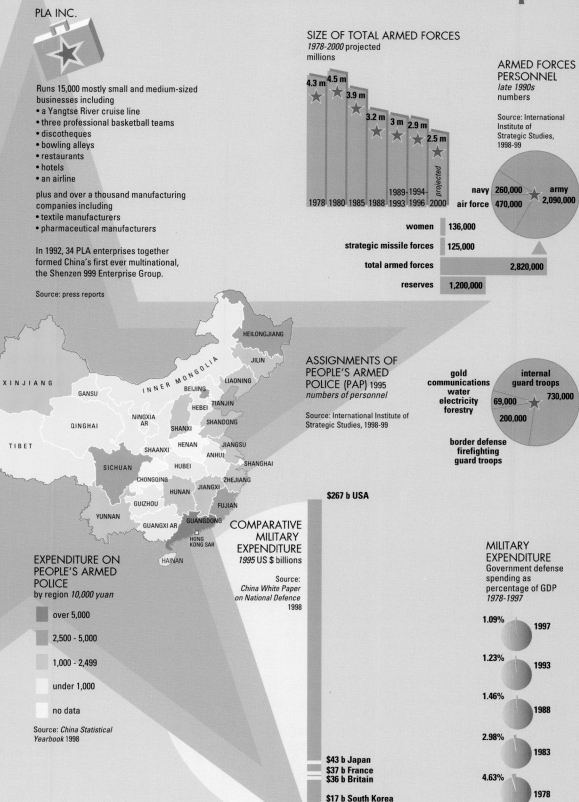

PLA INC.

Runs 15,000 mostly small and medium-sized businesses including
- a Yangtse River cruise line
- three professional basketball teams
- discotheques
- bowling alleys
- restaurants
- hotels
- an airline

plus and over a thousand manufacturing companies including
- textile manufacturers
- pharmaceutical manufacturers

In 1992, 34 PLA enterprises together formed China's first ever multinational, the Shenzen 999 Enterprise Group.

Source: press reports

SIZE OF TOTAL ARMED FORCES
1978-2000 projected
millions

4.3 m   4.5 m   3.9 m   3.2 m   3 m   2.9 m   2.5 m projected

1978   1980   1985   1988   1989-1993   1994-1996   2000

ARMED FORCES PERSONNEL
late 1990s
numbers

Source: International Institute of Strategic Studies, 1998-99

navy 260,000   army 2,090,000
air force 470,000

women	136,000
strategic missile forces	125,000
total armed forces	2,820,000
reserves	1,200,000

ASSIGNMENTS OF PEOPLE'S ARMED POLICE (PAP) 1995
numbers of personnel

Source: International Institute of Strategic Studies, 1998-99

gold communications water electricity forestry   69,000
internal guard troops 730,000
200,000
border defense firefighting guard troops

EXPENDITURE ON PEOPLE'S ARMED POLICE
by region *10,000 yuan*

- over 5,000
- 2,500 - 5,000
- 1,000 - 2,499
- under 1,000
- no data

Source: *China Statistical Yearbook* 1998

COMPARATIVE MILITARY EXPENDITURE
1995 US $ billions

Source: *China White Paper on National Defence* 1998

$267 b USA
$43 b Japan
$37 b France
$36 b Britain
$17 b South Korea
$16 b Russia
$10 b China

MILITARY EXPENDITURE
Government defense spending as percentage of GDP *1978-1997*

1.09%   1997
1.23%   1993
1.46%   1988
2.98%   1983
4.63%   1978

RATHER BE A BROKEN JADE THAN A WHOLE TILE

China wants to be taken seriously in world affairs. It wants to be a part of the community of nations – a member of international organizations such as the World Trade Organization – as well as a regional and world military power.

The end of the cold war, the collapse of the former USSR and the relative success of China's economy, in contrast with the 1997-98 Asian economic crisis, have enhanced the country's power base. However, disputes with the USA over nuclear test programs, missile sales, human rights' abuses, and claims to "indisputable sovereignty" over Taiwan have undermined China's influence in the world. In the Asia-Pacific region, tension is heightened further by China's refusal to eschew the use of force in its claims to, as well as Taiwan, the Paracel (Xisha) and Spratly (Nansha) islands.

MILITARY IMBALANCE
China and Taiwan
late 1990s numbers

Sources: IISS, 1998-99; press reports

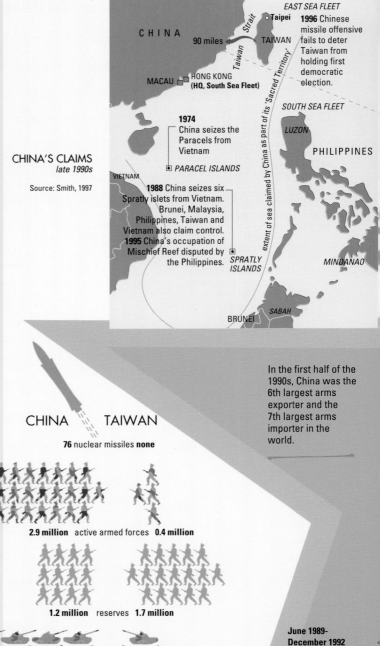

CHINA'S CLAIMS
late 1990s

Source: Smith, 1997

1996 Chinese missile offensive fails to deter Taiwan from holding first democratic election.

1974 China seizes the Paracels from Vietnam

1988 China seizes six Spratly islets from Vietnam. Brunei, Malaysia, Philippines, Taiwan and Vietnam also claim control.
1995 China's occupation of Mischief Reef disputed by the Philippines.

CHINA   TAIWAN

76 nuclear missiles **none**

2.9 million   active armed forces   0.4 million

1.2 million   reserves   1.7 million

16,300   battletanks and other armed vehicles   3,349

3,566   combat aircraft   529

863   naval forces   141

In the first half of the 1990s, China was the 6th largest arms exporter and the 7th largest arms importer in the world.

June 1989- December 1992 President Bush boosts trade despite Tiananmen crackdown.

January-May 1993 President Clinton restores link between human rights and trade.

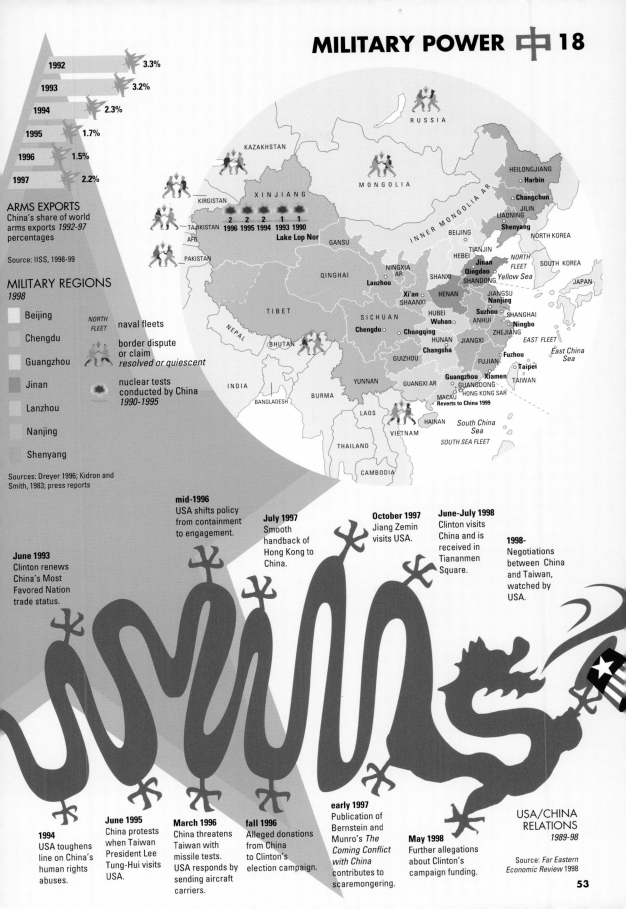

1992	3.3%
1993	3.2%
1994	2.3%
1995	1.7%
1996	1.5%
1997	2.2%

ARMS EXPORTS
China's share of world arms exports *1992-97* percentages

Source: IISS, 1998-99

MILITARY REGIONS
1998

- Beijing
- Chengdu
- Guangzhou
- Jinan
- Lanzhou
- Nanjing
- Shenyang

NORTH FLEET — naval fleets

border dispute or claim *resolved or quiescent*

nuclear tests conducted by China *1990-1995*

Sources: Dreyer 1996; Kidron and Smith, 1983; press reports

Map labels

RUSSIA

KAZAKHSTAN

MONGOLIA

KIRGISTAN

XINJIANG

TAJIKISTAN

AFG

PAKISTAN

2 2 2 1 1
1996 1995 1994 1993 1990
Lake Lop Nor

GANSU

QINGHAI

TIBET

NEPAL

BHUTAN

INDIA

BANGLADESH

BURMA

LAOS

THAILAND

CAMBODIA

VIETNAM

HAINAN

YUNNAN

GUANGXI AR

GUIZHOU

SICHUAN

Chengdu

Chongqing

HUNAN

Changsha

JIANGXI

GUANGDONG

Guangzhou

MACAU
Reverts to China 1999

HONG KONG SAR

FUJIAN

Fuzhou

Xiamen

Taipei

TAIWAN

NINGXIA AR

Lanzhou

SHAANXI

Xi'an

HENAN

HUBEI

Wuhan

INNER MONGOLIA AR

BEIJING

HEBEI

TIANJIN

SHANXI

SHANDONG

Jinan

Qingdao

Yellow Sea

NORTH FLEET

JIANGSU

Nanjing

ANHUI

Suzhou

SHANGHAI

ZHEJIANG

Ningbo

EAST FLEET

East China Sea

HEILONGJIANG

Harbin

Changchun

JILIN

LIAONING

Shenyang

NORTH KOREA

SOUTH KOREA

JAPAN

South China Sea

SOUTH SEA FLEET

USA/CHINA RELATIONS
1989-98

Source: *Far Eastern Economic Review* 1998

June 1993
Clinton renews China's Most Favored Nation trade status.

mid-1996
USA shifts policy from containment to engagement.

July 1997
Smooth handback of Hong Kong to China.

October 1997
Jiang Zemin visits USA.

June-July 1998
Clinton visits China and is received in Tiananmen Square.

1998-
Negotiations between China and Taiwan, watched by USA.

1994
USA toughens line on China's human rights abuses.

June 1995
China protests when Taiwan President Lee Tung-Hui visits USA.

March 1996
China threatens Taiwan with missile tests. USA responds by sending aircraft carriers.

fall 1996
Alleged donations from China to Clinton's election campaign.

early 1997
Publication of Bernstein and Munro's *The Coming Conflict with China* contributes to scaremongering.

May 1998
Further allegations about Clinton's campaign funding.

CAN TWO TIGERS LIVE ON THE SAME MOUNTAIN?

Beijing and Shanghai, along with Tianjin and - since 1997 - Chongqing, are the four cities in China with the same status as provinces.

While Beijing ranks as the political capital, and the cultural and educational center, Shanghai is not content simply to restore its reputation as the Paris of the East. The birthplace of China's Communist Party, Shanghai is striving to be the citadel of its socialist market economy. The engine behind this drive is the construction of the Pudong Special Economic Zone across the Huangpu River from Shanghai's historic Bund. If successful, Shanghai will become China's financial, as well as industrial, center.

No longer a construction site employing one quarter of the world's cranes, Pudong's skyline is rising as a new city, some say, to rival Hong Kong. Yet much of Shanghai's development is financed by Hong Kong property developers. A more likely competition is the construction of the world's tallest building.

12.8 million population

2,480 people per square km density

181,000 million yuan GDP

16,735 yuan GDP per person

11,019 yuan average wage

6.6 million employed

unemployed **71,500**

US $5,834 million exports

US $9,786 million imports

direct foreign investment **US $1,592 million**

investment in new construction **1,801 million yuan**

105,150 million yuan retail sales

US $2,248 million tourist revenue

338 hotels

54,094 taxis

136 per km cars

4 per 100 households motorbikes

209 per 100 households bicycles

124 per 100 households color TVs

56 per 100 households VCRs

10 per 100 households VCDs

12 per 100 households computers

Beijing

population **14.9 million**

density **people per square km** 3,853

GDP **336,000 million yuan**

GDP per person **25,750 yuan**

average wage **11,425 yuan**

employed **7.7 million**

unemployed **298,200**

exports **US $14,767 million**

imports **US $15,598 million**

direct foreign investment **US $4,225 million**

investment in new construction **1,081 million yuan**

retail sales **132,520 million yuan**

tourist revenue **US $1,317 million**

hotels **127**

taxis **40,997**

cars **122 per km**

motorbikes **per 100 households 2**

bicycles **per 100 households 125**

color TVs **per 100 households 119**

VCRs **per 100 households 52**

VCDs **per 100 households 15**

computers **per 100 households 9**

Sources: *China Labor Statistical Yearbook* 1997; *China Statistical Yearbook* 1998

○ **Shanghai**

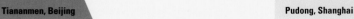

Tiananmen, Beijing

Pudong, Shanghai

THE MOUNTAINS ARE HIGH AND THE EMPEROR IS FAR AWAY

The coastal provinces are taking the lion's share of foreign direct investment. In 1997, this amounted to 89 percent of the total, increasing economic inequality between the regions and demonstrating the power of these provinces relative to central government. The extra-budgetary revenues, sometimes known as the "second budget", are an important source of local power. There are many different fees, including fees for every pig slaughtered, for animal innoculations, for school, for permits to marry or to have a baby.

Party and government structures run in parallel, extending down from the center to the grassroots where village committes are elected throughout China.

ORGANIZATION OF COMMUNIST PARTY

Source: authors

SHARES OF REVENUE AND EXPENDITURE
total government and central government shares as percentage of GNP *1981 and 1997*

Source: *China Statistical Yearbook* 1998

	1981	1997
total government revenue	24.2	11.8
central government revenue	6.4	5.8
total government expenditure	23.4	12.6
central government expenditure	12.9	3.4

THE SECOND BUDGET
central and local shares of extra-budgetary revenue and expenditure (fees, charges and local taxes) as a percentage of budgetary revenue

Source: *China Statistical Yearbook* 1998

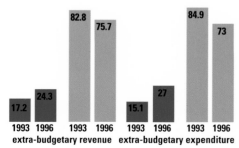

	central government	local government
extra-budgetary revenue 1993	17.2	82.8
extra-budgetary revenue 1996	24.3	75.7
extra-budgetary expenditure 1993	15.1	84.9
extra-budgetary expenditure 1996	27	73

PROVINCIAL POWER
Shares of foreign direct investment (FDI) *1991-1997*

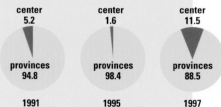

	1991	1995	1997
center	5.2	1.6	11.5
provinces	94.8	98.4	88.5

Source: *China Statistical Yearbook* 1998

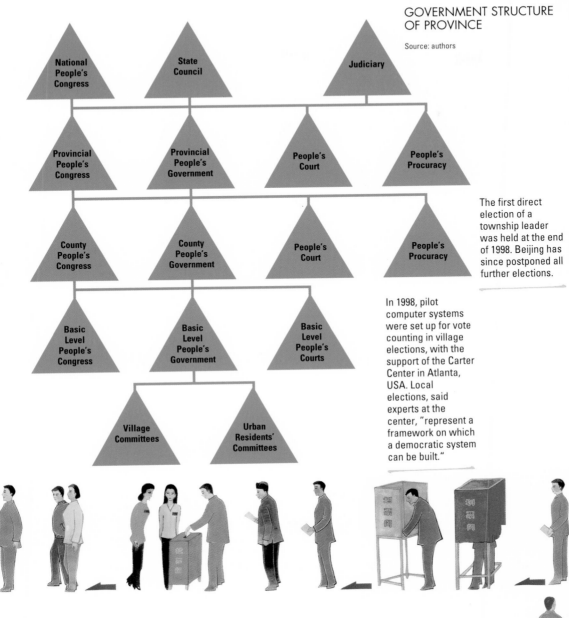

GOVERNMENT STRUCTURE OF PROVINCE

Source: authors

National People's Congress

State Council

Judiciary

Provincial People's Congress

Provincial People's Government

People's Court

People's Procuracy

County People's Congress

County People's Government

People's Court

People's Procuracy

Basic Level People's Congress

Basic Level People's Government

Basic Level People's Courts

Village Committees

Urban Residents' Committees

The first direct election of a township leader was held at the end of 1998. Beijing has since postponed all further elections.

In 1998, pilot computer systems were set up for vote counting in village elections, with the support of the Carter Center in Atlanta, USA. Local elections, said experts at the center, "represent a framework on which a democratic system can be built."

THE VILLAGE

AIMS
democratic elections
democratic management
democratic policy-making
democratic supervision

ELECTIONS
China's 932,000 villages are strong in the northeast and southern coastal regions but weak in the north and west. Between 1988 and 1996 there have been three village committee elections, including some by secret ballot. 21 provinces participated in all three elections.

COMMITTEE MEMBERS
Committees have 4-7 members, of which at least one must be a woman. In large villages assemblies have one representative for about every 10 households. In other villages, everyone can attend the assembly.

MOUNTAINS AND RIVERS ARE EASY TO MOVE BUT IT IS IMPOSSIBLE TO CHANGE THE NATURE OF A MAN

China in the era of economic reform has taken an important step towards legality, moving away from the Maoist principle of rule by persons to rule by law and towards enshrining the rule of law in the Constitution.

Market and property relations require formal procedures and rules. While mediation remains an important means of settling domestic conflicts, the number of economic disputes coming before the courts is significantly increasing. At the same time, *guanxi* or using informal contacts is embedded in China's economic, political, and social life. Although *guanxi* may benefit those with personal ties, authority is eroded and enforcement is undermined. Corruption flourishes in this environment.

most corrupt

CORRUPTION
Perceived illicit payments or other bribes made to elected or appointed officials, or to employees of public agencies and companies *1997* index of 52 countries ranked from 0 to 10

Source: *Far Eastern Economic Review* 1997

52	8.34 Nigeria
49	7.73 Russia
48	7.47 Pakistan
46	7.28 Indonesia
45	7.25 India
41	★ 7.12 China
40	6.95 Philippines
39	6.94 Thailand
34	5.71 South Korea
32	4.99 Malaysia
31	4.98 Taiwan
21	3.43 Japan
18	2.72 Hong Kong
16	2.39 USA
9	1.34 Singapore
1	0.06 Denmark

least corrupt

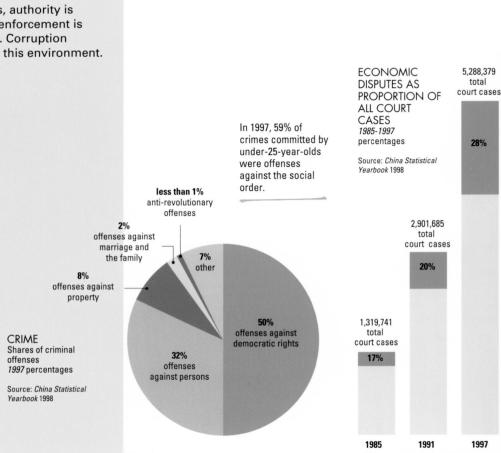

ECONOMIC DISPUTES AS PROPORTION OF ALL COURT CASES
1985-1997 percentages

Source: *China Statistical Yearbook* 1998

5,288,379 total court cases — 28%

2,901,685 total court cases — 20%

1,319,741 total court cases — 17%

1985   1991   1997

In 1997, 59% of crimes committed by under-25-year-olds were offenses against the social order.

less than 1% anti-revolutionary offenses

2% offenses against marriage and the family

8% offenses against property

7% other

50% offenses against democratic rights

32% offenses against persons

CRIME
Shares of criminal offenses *1997* percentages

Source: *China Statistical Yearbook* 1998

LAW INFORCEMENT EXPENDITURE
Public security and armed police expenditure compared with welfare expenditure *1997*

- over five times as much is spent on security
- over three times as much
- over twice as much
- up to twice as much
- no data

Source: *China Statistical Yearbook* 1998

LEGAL SYSTEM

Source: *Information China* 1989

I N J I A N G

GANSU

INNER MONGOLIA AR

HEILONGJIANG

JILIN

LIAONING

BEIJING

TIANJIN

HEBEI

NINGXIA AR

QINGHAI

SHANXI

SHANDONG

SHAANXI

HENAN

JIANGSU

TIBET

SICHUAN

CHONGQING

HUBEI

ANHUI

SHANGHAI

ZHEJIANG

JIANGXI

HUNAN

GUIZHOU

FUJIAN

TAIWAN

YUNNAN

GUANGXI AR

GUANGDONG

HONG KONG SAR

MACAU

HAINAN

CONSTITUTION
modified by the National People's Congress

FUNDAMENTAL LAWS
enacted and modified by the National People's Congress

LAWS
enacted and modified by the Standing Committee of the National People's Congress

ADMINISTRATIVE RULES AND REGULATIONS
enacted and revised by the State Council

REGULATIONS
made by Ministries or Committees of the State Council

LOCAL RULES AND REGULATIONS
enacted and revised by the People's Congress and its Standing Committee of Provinces, Autonomous Regions or Municipalities directly under the central government

There were over 3 million civil court settlements in 1997. Over half were settled through mediation.

MEDIATION
Proportion of civil cases settled in court through mediation *1997*

Source: *China Statistical Yearbook* 1998

RULES AND REGULATIONS
made by the People's Government of Provinces, Autonomous Regions and Municipalities directly under the central government

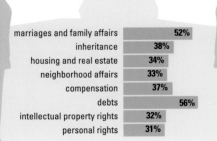

marriages and family affairs	52%
inheritance	38%
housing and real estate	34%
neighborhood affairs	33%
compensation	37%
debts	56%
intellectual property rights	32%
personal rights	31%

KILL THE CHICKENS TO SCARE THE MONKEYS

China takes the principles of human rights seriously. The Constitution provides a full listing and accords them priority. China has endorsed the UN Convention on Political and Civil Rights. Practice, however, defies international principles. Throughout the 1990s more people were executed in China than in the rest of the world put together. Even if the official figures on which the map is based are an underestimate, as Amnesty International argues, the "strike hard" campaign of 1996-97 was particularly brutal.

More positively, the growth of civil society with associations and groups acting as intermediaries between the state and citizens may be strengthened by the announcement that private social organizations, but not political parties, may seek government approval.

HUMAN RIGHTS' ABUSERS
selected countries *1998*

Scores based on human rights' violations including: extrajudicial killings, death penalty, torture, disappearances, denial of free speech and of political, women's religious, minority, and children's rights.

Rank out of 194 countries

Source: *The Observer Human Rights Index*, 1998

EXECUTIONS
Number per month
1992-97

Source: *Far Eastern Economic Review*, 1998

1992	1994	1995	1996	1997
90	171	211	1,000	156

In a spirit of legal reform in 1998, China published statistics on the numbers tortured and murdered by police.

Scores

Scores	111	103	100	96	95	84	83	82	80	78	40	38	37	31	24
Rank	1	2	3	4	5	6	7	8	9	10	47	54	56	73	99
	Algeria	North Korea	Burma	Indonesia	Libya	Colombia	Syria	Iraq	Yugoslavia	China	Taiwan	Malaysia	South Korea	Hong Kong	Singapore

SHARES OF EXECUTIONS BY CRIME COMMITED
1997 percentages

Source: Amnesty International, 1998

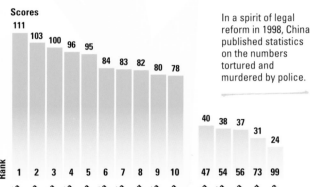

- bombing 1%
- prostitution/ abduction 3%
- assault 2%
- theft 5%
- rape 1%
- guns < 1%
- miscellaneous 2%
- hooliganism 2%
- economic 4%
- Unknown 14%
- robbery 17%
- murder 21%
- drugs 27%

CITIZENS' ORGANIZATIONS

Source: White, 1996

PILLAR ORGANIZATION
Young Communist League

PILLAR ORGANIZATION
All-China Federation of Trade Unions

PILLAR ORGANIZATION
Women's Federation

UNDERGROUND ORGANIZATIONS
democracy movement, religious groups

UNOFFICIAL ORGANIZATIONS
environmental groups, women's groups

OFFICIALLY RECOGNIZED SOCIAL ORGANIZATIONS
such as the Lawyers' Association, Calligraphers' Association

PARTY STATE

THE DEATH PENALTY
Publicly-reported death sentences and executions
1997

Amnesty International recorded 3,152 death sentences and 1,876 confirmed executions in China in 1997.

Source: Amnesty International, 1998

- up to 50 death sentences
- 50 to 100
- 100 to 200
- 200 to 500 death sentences

number of executions

HEILONGJIANG 38
11
JILIN 2
XINJIANG 88
INNER MONGOLIA AR
GANSU
64
•BEIJING
58 LIAONING
35
TIANJIN
HEBEI
8
NINGXIA AR
QINGHAI 1
94 68
SHANXI
SHANDONG 7
42
TIBET
31
SHAANXI
HENAN 42
JIANGSU
4
71 26 42
SICHUAN
CHONGQING
HUBEI 86
ANHUI
SHANGHAI
ZHEJIANG
185
JIANGXI 8
6
HUNAN
GUIZHOU 21
28 67 FUJIAN
YUNNAN
GUANGXI
GUANGDONG
TAIWAN
198
44
361
HONG KONG SAR
MACAU
HAINAN 70

Yellow River
Yangtse River

INTELLECTUAL FREEDOM
1998

Source: *Far Eastern Economic Review*, 1998

1957 ONE HUNDRED FLOWERS
Invited by Mao Zedong to criticize the Communist Party, Chinese intellectuals attack its right to govern. Many are punished by exile to the countryside.

1978-79 DEMOCRACY WALL
Deng Xiaoping encourages citizens to paste political tracts on a Beijing wall. Wei Jingsheng accuses him of tyranny and is arrested. Wall closed.

1982-83 SPIRITUAL POLLUTION
Deng cracks down on greater personal freedoms demanded by People's Daily editor and others.

1986 BOURGEOIS LIBERALISM
Deng's renewed interest in administrative reform encourages students to demand more freedom from Communist Party control. Reformist party chief Hu Yaobang sacked.

1989 TIANANMEN MASSACRE
Party split between leftists and reformers. Deng orders troops to attack students demonstrating for more freedom. Reformist party chief Zhao Ziyang sacked.

1994 RIGHT AND LEFT
Neoconservatives, like leftists, call for tighter central control of economy and provinces.

1998 NEW LIBERALISM
Liberals attack neoconservatives and leftists, calling for greater political freedom and curbs on Communist Party power.

The government's attempt to censor and control political news on the internet has distracted attention from its massive investment in telecommunications' infrastructure.
By 2000, the number of internet users in China is expected to be second only to the number in the USA.

Part Four

THE STATE AND SOCIETY

IDEOLOGY CANNOT SUPPLY RICE

An internal State Land Bureau estimate predicts that China has 40 percent more arable land than the official figure given by the state Statistical Bureau. The higher arable land figure, combined with steady increases in productivity owing to improved plant varieties, and family planning, should enable China to meet its food needs when the population peaks at a projected 1.6 billion during the 2030s.

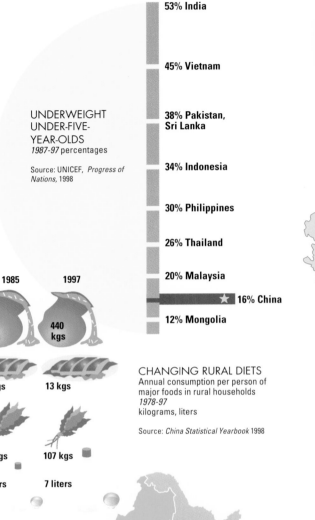

UNDERWEIGHT UNDER-FIVE-YEAR-OLDS
1987-97 percentages

Source: UNICEF, *Progress of Nations,* 1998

53% India

45% Vietnam

38% Pakistan, Sri Lanka

34% Indonesia

30% Philippines

26% Thailand

20% Malaysia

★ 16% China

12% Mongolia

	1978	1985	1997
grain	371 kgs	466 kgs	440 kgs
pork beef mutton	6 kgs	11 kgs	13 kgs
fresh vegetables	142 kgs	131 kgs	107 kgs
liquor	1 liter	4 liters	7 liters

CHANGING RURAL DIETS
Annual consumption per person of major foods in rural households
1978-97
kilograms, liters

Source: *China Statistical Yearbook* 1998

RURAL EXPENDITURE ON FOOD
as a percentage of living expenditure *1998*

- 60% and over
- 55-59%
- 50-54%
- 45-49%
- under 45%
- no data

Source: *China Statistical Yearbook* 1998

HEILONGJIANG
JILIN
XINJIANG
INNER MONGOLIA
LIAONING
BEIJING
GANSU
TIANJIN
HEBEI
NINGXIA AR
SHANXI
SHANDONG
QINGHAI
SHAANXI
HENAN
JIANGSU
TIBET
SICHUAN
ANHUI
SHANGHAI
HUBEI
CHONGQING
ZHEJIANG
HUNAN
JIANGXI
GUIZHOU
FUJIAN
YUNNAN
GUANGXI AR
GUANGDONG
TAIWAN
HONG KONG SAR
HAINAN

Fastfood outlets in China are becoming more popular than traditional restaurants.

URBAN EXPENDITURE ON FOOD
as a percentage of living expenditure *1998*

- 55-59%
- 50-54%
- 45-49%
- under 45%
- no data

Source: *China Statistical Yearbook* 1998

DINING OUT
as a percentage of expenditure on food

- 12% and over
- 6-11%
- under 6%

XINJIANG

GANSU

INNER MONGOLIA AR

HEILONGJIANG

JILIN

LIAONING

BEIJING

TIANJIN

NINGXIA AR

HEBEI

SHANDONG

QINGHAI

SHANXI

SHAANXI

JIANGSU

HENAN

TIBET

ANHUI

SHANGHAI

HUBEI

CHONGQING

ZHEJIANG

SICHUAN

JIANGXI

HUNAN

FUJIAN

GUIZHOU

YUNNAN

GUANGXI AR

GUANGDONG

TAIWAN

MACAU

HONG KONG SAR

HAINAN

FISH PRODUCTION
1978-97 1,000 tonnes

Source: *China Statistical Yearbook* 1998

CHINESE CUISINE
The Four Styles

Source: authors

duck

SHANDONG

SICHUAN

carp

JIANGSU

pepper

GUANGDONG

wintermelon

	1978	1985	1997
wild sea water	3,145	3,485	13,853
farmed sea water	45	712	7,910
wild fresh water	293	476	1,786
farmed fresh water	762	2,378	12,376

EATING IN THE EAST, SLEEPING IN THE WEST

China's households are changing in response to new social norms and economic demands. One-child families are the rule in cities. High divorce rates are breaking down the traditional family. Urban dwellers still occupy less living space than those who live in the countryside, and many families share cooking and bathroom facilities. The urban trend towards single-income households is squeezing women out of the labor market.

THE GENERATIONS
Share of population living in one, two and three generation households
1995
percentages

Source: *China Population Statistics Yearbook* 1997

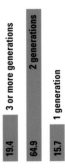

3 or more generations — **19.4**
2 generations — **64.9**
1 generation — **15.7**

One-child family life is often dominated by precocious, spoilt "Little Emperors" and "Empresses" who can recite Tang poetry but are unable to tie their own shoelaces.

CHOICE OF MARRIAGE PARTNER IN RURAL CHINA
Anhui province *early 1980s*

Source: Mackerras , 1997

free choice — **15%**
arranged by parents — **10%**
arranged by parents and "agreed" by partners — **75%**

In urban marriages, the pattern is reversed: 75% free choice; 10% "agreed"

In 1995, thirty-five percent of marriages involved at least one partner who was below the legal minimum age: 20 years old for women and 22 for men.

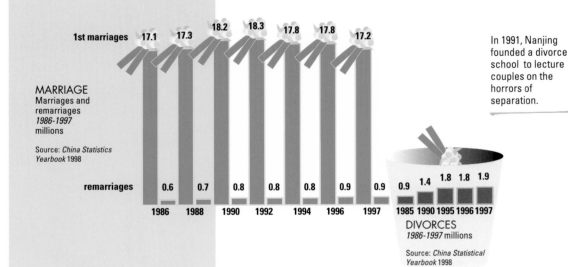

1st marriages 17.1 17.3 18.2 18.3 17.8 17.8 17.2

MARRIAGE
Marriages and remarriages
1986-1997
millions

Source: *China Statistics Yearbook* 1998

remarriages 0.6 0.7 0.8 0.8 0.8 0.9 0.9

1986 1988 1990 1992 1994 1996 1997

0.9 1.4 1.8 1.8 1.9

1985 1990 1995 1996 1997

DIVORCES
1986-1997 millions

Source: *China Statistical Yearbook* 1998

In 1991, Nanjing founded a divorce school to lecture couples on the horrors of separation.

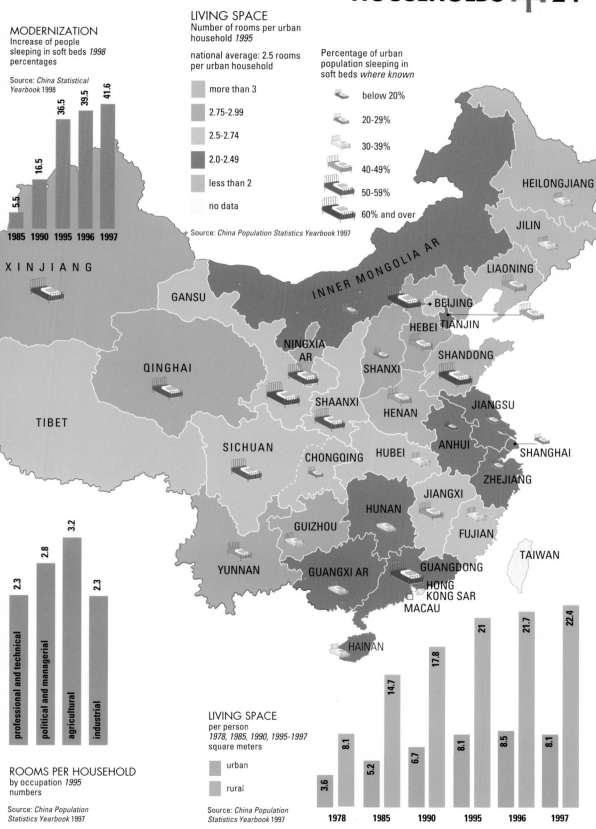

MODERNIZATION
Increase of people
sleeping in soft beds *1998*
percentages

Source: *China Statistical
Yearbook* 1998

Bar chart:
- 1985: 5.5
- 1990: 16.5
- 1995: 36.5
- 1996: 39.5
- 1997: 41.6

LIVING SPACE
Number of rooms per urban
household *1995*

national average: 2.5 rooms
per urban household

- more than 3
- 2.75-2.99
- 2.5-2.74
- 2.0-2.49
- less than 2
- no data

Percentage of urban
population sleeping in
soft beds *where known*

- below 20%
- 20-29%
- 30-39%
- 40-49%
- 50-59%
- 60% and over

Source: *China Population Statistics Yearbook* 1997

Map labels: XINJIANG, GANSU, INNER MONGOLIA AR, HEILONGJIANG, JILIN, LIAONING, BEIJING, HEBEI, TIANJIN, SHANDONG, QINGHAI, NINGXIA AR, SHANXI, SHAANXI, HENAN, JIANGSU, TIBET, SICHUAN, CHONGQING, HUBEI, ANHUI, SHANGHAI, ZHEJIANG, JIANGXI, HUNAN, GUIZHOU, FUJIAN, TAIWAN, YUNNAN, GUANGXI AR, GUANGDONG, HONG KONG SAR, MACAU, HAINAN

ROOMS PER HOUSEHOLD
by occupation *1995*
numbers

Bar chart:
- professional and technical: 2.3
- political and managerial: 2.8
- agricultural: 3.2
- industrial: 2.3

Source: *China Population
Statistics Yearbook* 1997

LIVING SPACE
per person
1978, 1985, 1990, 1995-1997
square meters

- urban
- rural

Source: *China Population
Statistics Yearbook* 1997

Bar chart:
- 1978: rural 3.6, urban 8.1
- 1985: rural 5.2, urban 8.1
- 1990: rural 6.7, urban 17.8
- 1995: rural 8.1, urban 21
- 1996: rural 8.5, urban 21.7
- 1997: rural 8.1, urban 22.4

GREAT VESSELS TAKE LONGER TO COMPLETE

China has made great strides in improving literacy. However, more than 150 million people are illiterate. Of these, 92 percent live in rural areas and over 70 percent are women.

Market reforms are making an impact on education in numerous ways. In a competitive environment, many urban Chinese children attend nursery schools from the age of one, and kindergarten between from three to six years old. Private schools and colleges are growing rapidly in affluent areas. As for state schools, 80 percent have to raise funds by setting up their own enterprises. The demand for Masters' degrees in Business Administration is growing rapidly.

1985 1995

1985	1995
France 5.4	7.6 France
Kenya 6.4	7.4 Kenya
Australia 5.6	5.6 Australia
UK 4.9	5.5 UK
USA 4.9	5.3 USA
	4.7 Germany
India 3.4	3.8 Japan
Hong Kong 2.8	3.5 India
China 2.9 ★	2.8 Hong Kong
most developed world 5	★ 2.3 China
less developed world 3.9	5.1 most developed world
least developed world 3	4.1 less developed world
	2.5 least developed world

EDUCATION SPENDING
Proportion of education spending as a percentage of GNP *1985 and 1995* selected countries percentages
Source: UNESCO *World Education Report* 1998

HIGHER EDUCATION
Shares of all students enroled in colleges and universities *1996* percentages

In 1996 there were over 1.000 colleges and universities in China, and 3 million students.

Eastern region 50%

Central region 32%

Western region 18%

Source: *China Statistical Yearbook 1997; China Regional Economy: A Profile of 17 Years of Reform and Opening-Up 1996*

Between 1979 and 1995, 220,000 students from mainland China studied abroad. By 1995, 75,000 had returned. By 1997, this number had risen to 90,000.

HIGH SCHOOLS
Graduates of junior secondary school (aged about 15) who go to senior secondary school *1995* percentages

national average: 48.8%
highest: Beijing 87.3%
lowest: Guangxi 18.6%

70% and over

60-69

50-59

40-49

30-39

below 30%

no data

Source: *China Regional Econo A Profile of 17 Years of Reform and Opening-Up 1996*

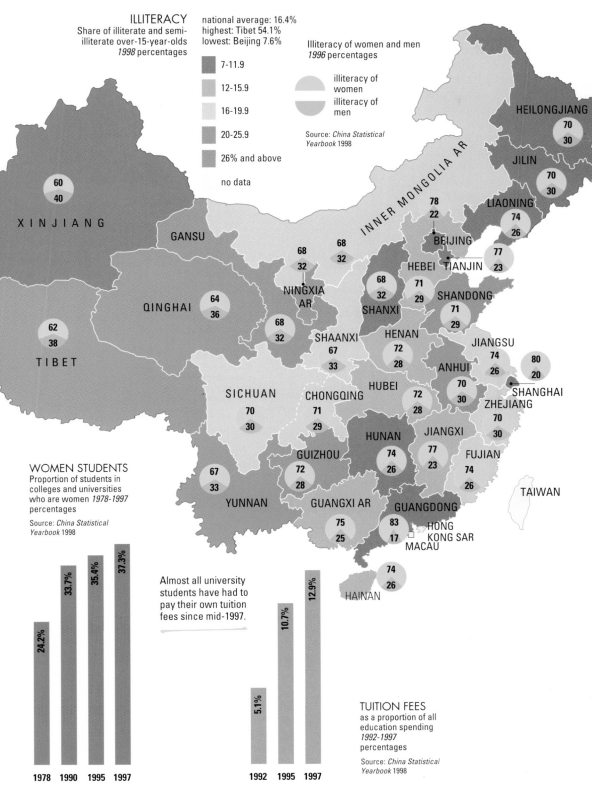

ILLITERACY
Share of illiterate and semi-illiterate over-15-year-olds *1998* percentages

national average: 16.4%
highest: Tibet 54.1%
lowest: Beijing 7.6%

- 7-11.9
- 12-15.9
- 16-19.9
- 20-25.9
- 26% and above
- no data

Illiteracy of women and men
1996 percentages

- illiteracy of women
- illiteracy of men

Source: *China Statistical Yearbook* 1998

XINJIANG 60 / 40
GANSU 68 / 32
INNER MONGOLIA AR 78 / 22
HEILONGJIANG 70 / 30
JILIN 70 / 30
LIAONING 74 / 26
BEIJING 68 / 32
HEBEI 71 / 29
TIANJIN 77 / 23
NINGXIA AR 68 / 32
SHANXI 68 / 32
SHANDONG 71 / 29
QINGHAI 64 / 36
TIBET 62 / 38
SHAANXI 67 / 33
HENAN 72 / 28
JIANGSU 74 / 26
SHANGHAI 80 / 20
ANHUI 70 / 30
HUBEI 72 / 28
ZHEJIANG 70 / 30
SICHUAN 70 / 30
CHONGQING 71 / 29
HUNAN 74 / 26
JIANGXI 77 / 23
FUJIAN 74 / 26
GUIZHOU 72 / 28
YUNNAN 67 / 33
GUANGXI AR 75 / 25
GUANGDONG 83 / 17
HONG KONG SAR
MACAU
HAINAN 74 / 26
TAIWAN

WOMEN STUDENTS
Proportion of students in colleges and universities who are women *1978-1997* percentages

Source: *China Statistical Yearbook* 1998

- 1978 — 24.2%
- 1990 — 33.7%
- 1995 — 35.4%
- 1997 — 37.3%

Almost all university students have had to pay their own tuition fees since mid-1997.

TUITION FEES
as a proportion of all education spending *1992-1997* percentages

Source: *China Statistical Yearbook* 1998

- 1992 — 5.1%
- 1995 — 10.7%
- 1997 — 12.9%

Robert Benewick and Stephanie Donald *The State of China Atlas* Copyright © Myriad Editions Limited

SUITING THE MEDICINE TO THE ILLNESS

Access to health care is increasingly a private matter. Collective or private enterprises do not offer medical cover for workers. State-owned enterprises, many of which are in financial difficulty, are finding it more difficult to meet the medical bills of their staff. In the countryside, health insurance is rare although more prosperous villages have set up their own schemes.

Both western and traditional medicine are widely practiced but, as elsewhere, medical personnel and facilities are distributed unevenly. Environment-related diseases are among the major killers. HIV cases are spreading rapidly.

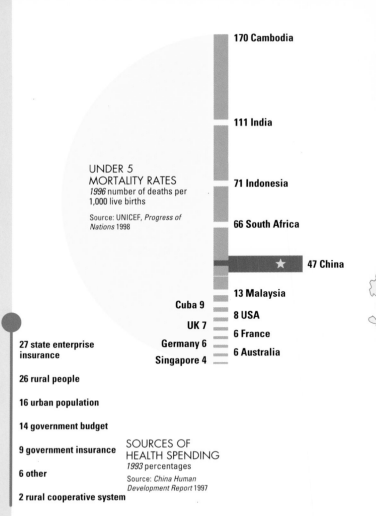

UNDER 5 MORTALITY RATES
1996 number of deaths per 1,000 live births

Source: UNICEF, *Progress of Nations* 1998

- 170 Cambodia
- 111 India
- 71 Indonesia
- 66 South Africa
- 47 China
- 13 Malaysia
- Cuba 9
- 8 USA
- UK 7
- 6 France
- Germany 6
- 6 Australia
- Singapore 4

SOURCES OF HEALTH SPENDING
1993 percentages

Source: *China Human Development Report* 1997

- 27 state enterprise insurance
- 26 rural people
- 16 urban population
- 14 government budget
- 9 government insurance
- 6 other
- 2 rural cooperative system

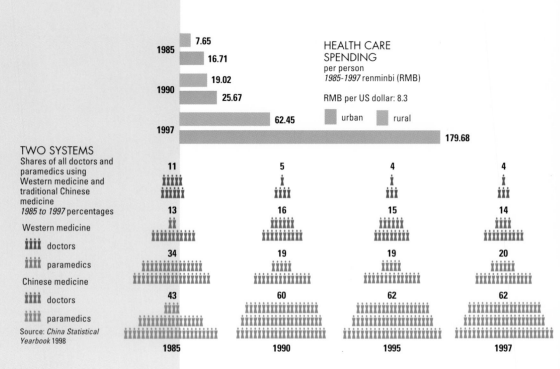

HEALTH CARE SPENDING
per person
1985-1997 renminbi (RMB)

RMB per US dollar: 8.3

urban   rural

1985	7.65
	16.71
1990	19.02
	25.67
1997	62.45
	179.68

TWO SYSTEMS
Shares of all doctors and paramedics using Western medicine and traditional Chinese medicine
1985 to 1997 percentages

Western medicine

👤 doctors

👤 paramedics

Chinese medicine

👤 doctors

👤 paramedics

Source: *China Statistical Yearbook* 1998

	1985	1990	1995	1997
Western doctors	11	5	4	4
Western paramedics	13	16	15	14
Chinese doctors	34	19	19	20
Chinese paramedics	43	60	62	62

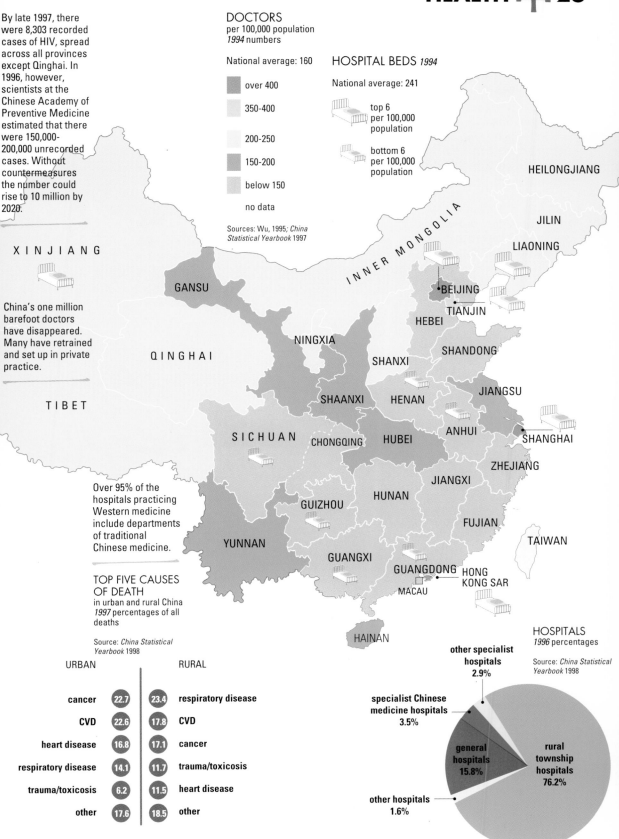

By late 1997, there were 8,303 recorded cases of HIV, spread across all provinces except Qinghai. In 1996, however, scientists at the Chinese Academy of Preventive Medicine estimated that there were 150,000-200,000 unrecorded cases. Without countermeasures the number could rise to 10 million by 2020.

China's one million barefoot doctors have disappeared. Many have retrained and set up in private practice.

Over 95% of the hospitals practicing Western medicine include departments of traditional Chinese medicine.

DOCTORS
per 100,000 population
1994 numbers

National average: 160

- over 400
- 350-400
- 200-250
- 150-200
- below 150
- no data

Sources: Wu, 1995; *China Statistical Yearbook* 1997

HOSPITAL BEDS *1994*

National average: 241

- top 6 per 100,000 population
- bottom 6 per 100,000 population

Map labels

XINJIANG
GANSU
QINGHAI
TIBET
NINGXIA
INNER MONGOLIA
HEILONGJIANG
JILIN
LIAONING
BEIJING
TIANJIN
HEBEI
SHANDONG
SHANXI
SHAANXI
HENAN
JIANGSU
SICHUAN
CHONGQING
HUBEI
ANHUI
SHANGHAI
ZHEJIANG
JIANGXI
GUIZHOU
HUNAN
FUJIAN
TAIWAN
YUNNAN
GUANGXI
GUANGDONG
HONG KONG SAR
MACAU
HAINAN

TOP FIVE CAUSES OF DEATH
in urban and rural China
1997 percentages of all deaths

Source: *China Statistical Yearbook* 1998

URBAN

cancer	22.7	
CVD	22.6	
heart disease	16.8	
respiratory disease	14.1	
trauma/toxicosis	6.2	
other	17.6	

RURAL

23.4	respiratory disease
17.8	CVD
17.1	cancer
11.7	trauma/toxicosis
11.5	heart disease
18.5	other

HOSPITALS
1996 percentages

Source: *China Statistical Yearbook* 1998

- other specialist hospitals 2.9%
- specialist Chinese medicine hospitals 3.5%
- general hospitals 15.8%
- rural township hospitals 76.2%
- other hospitals 1.6%

Robert Benewick and Stephanie Donald *The State of China Atlas* Copyright © Myriad Editions Limited

OPIUM OF THE PEOPLE

Despite the 1995 ban on cigarette advertising in China, the Chinese smoke 1.7 trillion cigarettes each year. Smuggling takes its place alongside habit and fashion in promoting smoking. A $2.50 pack of American cigarettes sells for a tax-free $1.00 on any city street.

Although the health costs to the government outweigh the revenues received, tobacco production is so integrated into the economy and smoking so much a part of urban male lifestyle as to defy easy solutions.

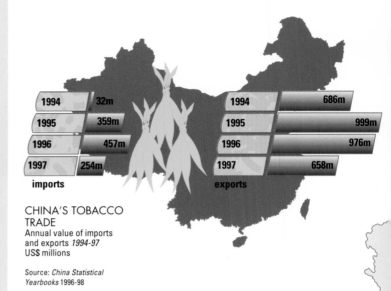

imports		exports	
1994	32m	1994	686m
1995	359m	1995	999m
1996	457m	1996	976m
1997	254m	1997	658m

CHINA'S TOBACCO TRADE
Annual value of imports and exports *1994-97*
US$ millions

Source: *China Statistical Yearbooks* 1996-98

SHARES OF WORLD TOBACCO EXPORTS
1998

Source: *China Statistical Yearbook* 1998

China **61%** USA **11%** Brazil **9%** India **8%** 3% Turkey 3% Zimbabwe 2% Malawi 2% Indonesia 2% Greece 2% Argentina

TOBACCO PRODUCTION
1997
10,000 cases per year

- 100
- 200-300
- over 600

Source: *China Statistical Yearbook* 1998

The Chinese tobacco industry employs 330,000 people.

Since 1978, the amount of farm land used for tobacco crops has tripled.

In the late 1990s, tobacco caused 12% of adult male deaths and 3% of adult female deaths in China.

If current smoking patterns persist, one third of all young men in China will eventually die as a result.

By 2050, tobacco will kill over 8,000 people each day and 3 million each year.

The number of women smoking appears to be decreasing.

SMOKING IN CHINA

Source: Liu, 1998

One in three of all cigarettes smoked in the world is smoked in China.

HEILONGJIANG
JILIN
LIAONING
XINJIANG
GANSU
INNER MONGOLIA AR
BEIJING
TIANJIN
HEBEI
NINGXIA AR
SHANXI
SHANDONG
QINGHAI
SHAANXI
HENAN
JIANGSU
TIBET
HUBEI
ANHUI
SHANGHAI
SICHUAN
ZHEJIANG
JIANGXI
HUNAN
GUIZHOU
FUJIAN
YUNNAN
GUANGXI AR
GUANGDONG
TAIWAN
HAINAN

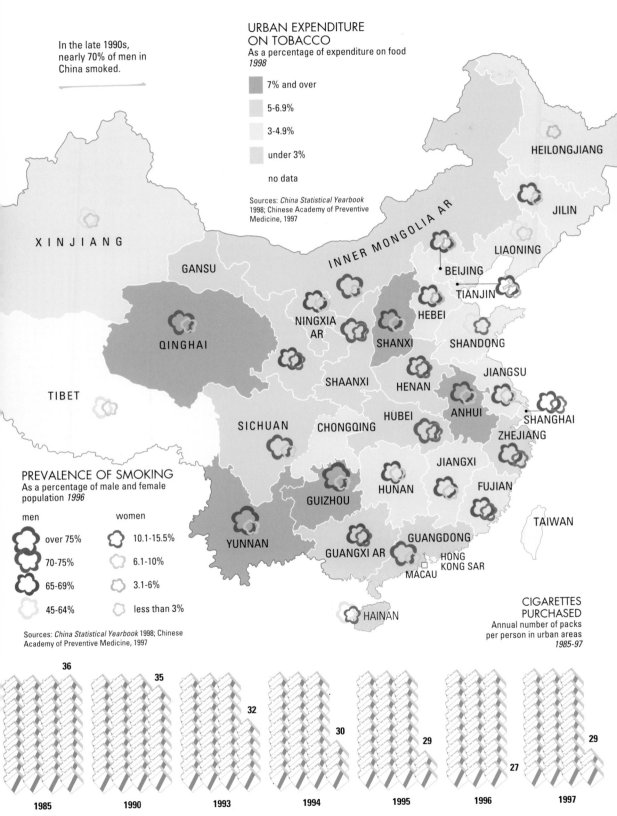

In the late 1990s, nearly 70% of men in China smoked.

URBAN EXPENDITURE ON TOBACCO
As a percentage of expenditure on food
1998

- 7% and over
- 5-6.9%
- 3-4.9%
- under 3%
- no data

Sources: *China Statistical Yearbook* 1998; Chinese Academy of Preventive Medicine, 1997

PREVALENCE OF SMOKING
As a percentage of male and female population *1996*

men
- over 75%
- 70-75%
- 65-69%
- 45-64%

women
- 10.1-15.5%
- 6.1-10%
- 3.1-6%
- less than 3%

Sources: *China Statistical Yearbook* 1998; Chinese Academy of Preventive Medicine, 1997

Map labels: XINJIANG, GANSU, INNER MONGOLIA AR, HEILONGJIANG, JILIN, LIAONING, BEIJING, TIANJIN, HEBEI, SHANDONG, NINGXIA AR, SHANXI, QINGHAI, TIBET, SHAANXI, HENAN, JIANGSU, ANHUI, SHANGHAI, ZHEJIANG, SICHUAN, CHONGQING, HUBEI, JIANGXI, FUJIAN, HUNAN, GUIZHOU, TAIWAN, YUNNAN, GUANGXI AR, GUANGDONG, HONG KONG SAR, MACAU, HAINAN

CIGARETTES PURCHASED
Annual number of packs per person in urban areas
1985-97

- **36** 1985
- **35** 1990
- **32** 1993
- **30** 1994
- **29** 1995
- **27** 1996
- **29** 1997

Robert Benewick and Stephanie Donald *The State of China Atlas* Copyright © Myriad Editions Limited

THE 1-2-4 PHENOMENON: ONE CHILD, TWO PARENTS, FOUR GRANDPARENTS

By 2030 China will have a higher percentage of older people than any other country except Sweden. Major social welfare reforms have been established with responsibility shifting towards the family. The new contribution-based social safety net replaces that provided by the state-owned enterprises.

By the end of 1996, 78 percent of urban workers – but only 6 percent of agricultural workers – had joined pension insurance schemes.

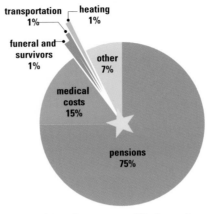

transportation 1% heating 1%

funeral and survivors 1%

other 7%

medical costs 15%

pensions 75%

Other allowances possible: for moving, difficult families, books and newspapers, and subsidies for non-staple foods, housing, water, electricity, bath house, barber.

SHARES OF SOCIAL WELFARE FUNDS
for retired workers from enterprises *1996* percentages

Source: *China Labor Statistical Yearbook* 1997

In 1997, according to official figures, the government spent 1.5% of its total budget on pensions and social welfare compared with 8.8% on defense.

RURAL WELFARE RELIEF *1995*

A government scheme for people with no other means of support. In 1995, fewer than 2.5 million met the stringent criteria applied.

clothing food and fuel housing

health burial

The Five Guarantees

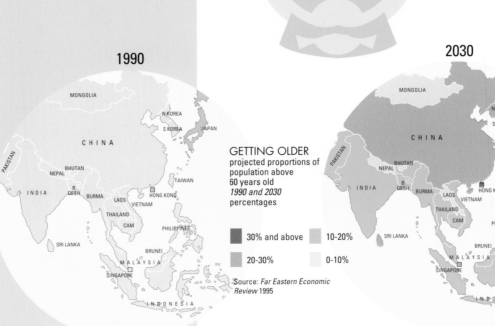

1990

2030

GETTING OLDER
projected proportions of population above 60 years old
1990 and 2030 percentages

- 30% and above
- 20-30%
- 10-20%
- 0-10%

Source: *Far Eastern Economic Review* 1995

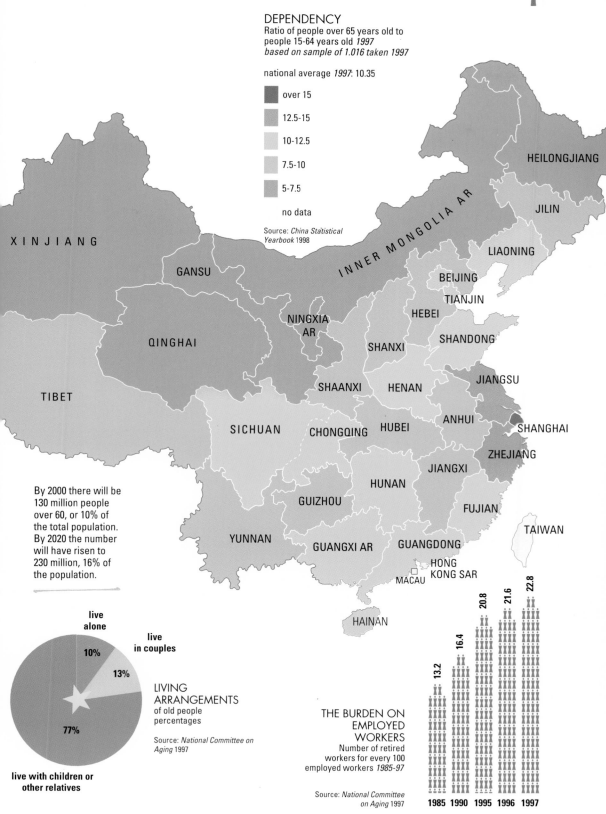

DEPENDENCY
Ratio of people over 65 years old to
people 15-64 years old *1997*
based on sample of 1.016 taken 1997

national average *1997*: 10.35

- over 15
- 12.5-15
- 10-12.5
- 7.5-10
- 5-7.5
- no data

Source: *China Statistical
Yearbook* 1998

XINJIANG

GANSU

INNER MONGOLIA AR

HEILONGJIANG

JILIN

LIAONING

BEIJING

TIANJIN

HEBEI

SHANDONG

NINGXIA
AR

QINGHAI

SHANXI

SHAANXI

HENAN

JIANGSU

TIBET

SICHUAN

CHONGQING

HUBEI

ANHUI

SHANGHAI

ZHEJIANG

JIANGXI

HUNAN

FUJIAN

TAIWAN

GUIZHOU

YUNNAN

GUANGXI AR

GUANGDONG

HONG
KONG SAR

MACAU

HAINAN

By 2000 there will be
130 million people
over 60, or 10% of
the total population.
By 2020 the number
will have risen to
230 million, 16% of
the population.

live alone

live in couples

10%

13%

77%

**LIVING
ARRANGEMENTS**
of old people
percentages

Source: *National Committee on
Aging* 1997

**live with children or
other relatives**

**THE BURDEN ON
EMPLOYED
WORKERS**
Number of retired
workers for every 100
employed workers *1985-97*

Source: *National Committee
on Aging* 1997

13.2
16.4
20.8
21.6
22.8

1985 1990 1995 1996 1997

MANDATES OF HEAVEN

Religions are tolerated in China under restricted conditions. Government regulations specify that no person shall use a religious venue for activities that might harm national or ethnic unity, social order, or citizens' health, or obstruct the national education system. Although missionaries are banned, in 1998 there were over 10,000 foreign Christian workers in China.

Monasteries and temples, devastated during the Cultural Revolution, are being restored.

HOLIDAYS AND FESTIVALS

250 m

RELIGIONS
estimates 1997

Sources: authors; press reports

Taoist/folk

Buddhists 68 m

Muslims 17 m

Protestant Christians 15 m

Catholics 4 m

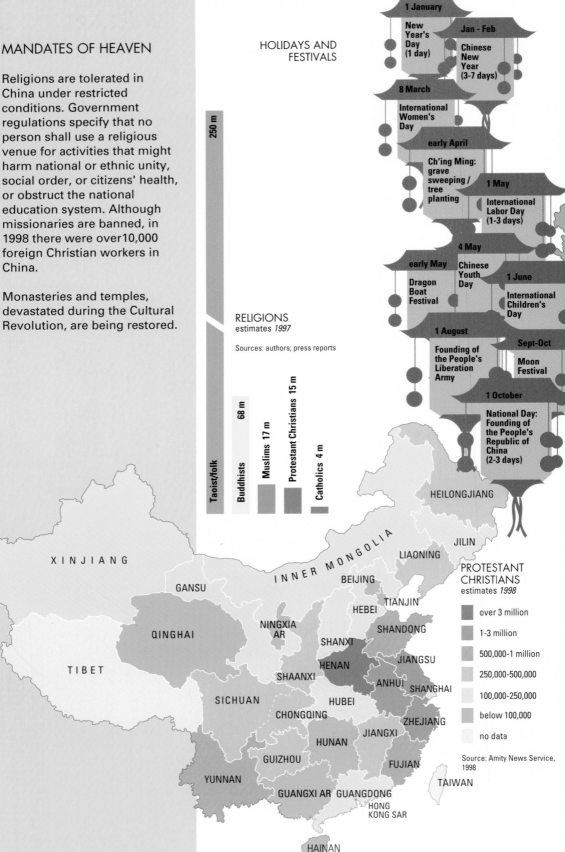

1 January
New Year's Day (1 day)

Jan - Feb
Chinese New Year (3-7 days)

8 March
International Women's Day

early April
Ch'ing Ming: grave sweeping / tree planting

1 May
International Labor Day (1-3 days)

4 May
Chinese Youth Day

early May
Dragon Boat Festival

1 June
International Children's Day

1 August
Founding of the People's Liberation Army

Sept-Oct
Moon Festival

1 October
National Day: Founding of the People's Republic of China (2-3 days)

HEILONGJIANG

JILIN

LIAONING

XINJIANG

GANSU

INNER MONGOLIA

BEIJING

TIANJIN

HEBEI

NINGXIA AR

SHANDONG

SHANXI

QINGHAI

SHAANXI

HENAN

JIANGSU

TIBET

ANHUI

SHANGHAI

SICHUAN

HUBEI

CHONGQING

ZHEJIANG

HUNAN

JIANGXI

GUIZHOU

FUJIAN

YUNNAN

TAIWAN

GUANGXI AR   GUANGDONG

HONG KONG SAR

HAINAN

PROTESTANT CHRISTIANS
estimates 1998

over 3 million

1-3 million

500,000-1 million

250,000-500,000

100,000-250,000

below 100,000

no data

Source: Amity News Service, 1998

SACRED SITES
Sites popular with tourists

major holy mountains

★ Communist Party sacred sites

Mao temple established 1993

Sources: O'Brien and Palmer
The State of Religion Atlas
1993; press reports

XINJIANG

GANSU

QINGHAI

TIBET

SICHUAN

YUNNAN

INNER MONGOLIA AR

HEILONGJIANG

JILIN

LIAONING

BEIJING

Beijing:
Tiananmen Square.
People's Republic of China
declared 1 October 1949

TIANJIN

Yellow River

Gushui:
Mao's temple
joins those of
other folk gods

Heng-shan
Taoist

SHANXI HEBEI

Wu-tai-shan
Buddhist

SHANDONG

NINGXIA AR

★

Yan'an:
Headquarters of liberated
areas 1936-49

Tai-shan
Taoist

JIANGSU

★ **Shanghai:**
National Congress
of Communist Party
of China 1921

SHANGHAI

SHAANXI

HENAN

ANHUI

HUBEI

Hua-shan
Taoist

Song-shan
Taoist

Jiuhua-shan
Buddhist

Pu-to
Island

CHONGQING

ZHEJIANG

Pu-to-shan
Buddhist

Himalayas
Buddhist and Hindu

Yangtse River

JIANGXI

Emei-shan
Buddhist

★

GUIZHOU

HUNAN

Heng-shan
Taoist

★ FUJIAN

Jinggang Mountains:
Jiangxi Soviet
established 1927

Zunyi Conference.
Mao takes
over leadership 1935

TAIWAN

YUNNAN

GUANGDONG

GUANGXI AR

★

Guangzhou:
Peasant Movement
Institute 1926

The leader of Tibetan Buddhism, the Dalai Lama operates a government in exile in Dharamsala, India. The 11th incarnation of the Panchen Lama, the second highest religious figure in Tibet, is a young boy being held by the Chinese government.

HAINAN

BUDDHISM
Location of the three main branches

Tibetan Buddhism

Chinese/Japanese Buddhism

Theravada Buddhism

Source: O'Brien and Palmer
The State of Religion Atlas
1993

Tuva Buryat

RUSSIA

MONGOLIA

KIR

N.KOREA

JAPAN

S.KOREA

Ladakh

CHINA

PAKISTAN

Tibet

NEPAL BHUTAN

B DESH

MACAU

TAIWAN

PACIFIC OCEAN

INDIA

BURMA

HONG KONG

Maharashtra

LAOS

THAILAND

CAM

VIETNAM

PHILIPPINES

SRI LANKA

BRUNEI

INDIAN OCEAN

MALAYSIA

ALTHOUGH WE LIVE SEPARATELY IN REMOTE CORNERS OF THE WORLD, WE FEEL LIKE FRIENDLY NEIGHBORS

China's increase in telephone mainlines during the 1980s and 1990s was the most rapid in the world. By 2000, it will have well over 100 million lines. Yet mobile phones are expected to take a larger share of the telecommunications market. Over 40 million subscribers are forecast by 2000, a rise of over 30 million in just three years.

China wants to insure its place in the global information-based economy. Efforts to boost the Chinese language presence on the internet through a low-cost domestic service will increase the number of Chinese users to ten million by 2003.

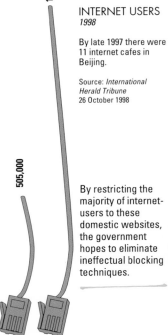

INTERNET USERS
1998

By late 1997 there were 11 internet cafes in Beijing.

Source: *International Herald Tribune* 26 October 1998

By restricting the majority of internet-users to these domestic websites, the government hopes to eliminate ineffectual blocking techniques.

1.2 m

505,000

early 1998 **October 1998**

mobile phones 12%

pagers 26%

main telephone lines 62%

SHARES OF TELEPHONE EQUIPMENT *1997*
percentages

Source: *China Statistical Yearbook* 1998

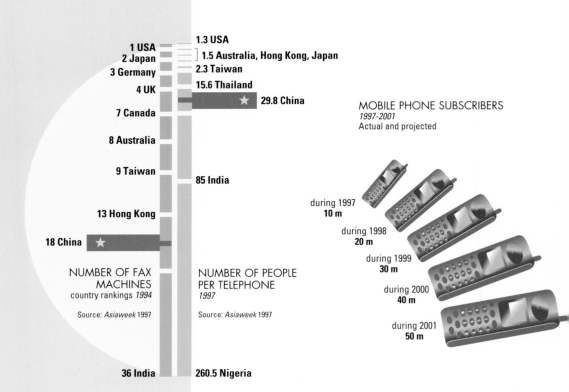

1 USA
2 Japan
3 Germany
4 UK
7 Canada
8 Australia
9 Taiwan
13 Hong Kong
18 China

NUMBER OF FAX MACHINES
country rankings *1994*

Source: *Asiaweek* 1997

36 India

1.3 USA
] 1.5 Australia, Hong Kong, Japan
2.3 Taiwan
15.6 Thailand
29.8 China

85 India

NUMBER OF PEOPLE PER TELEPHONE
1997

Source: *Asiaweek* 1997

260.5 Nigeria

MOBILE PHONE SUBSCRIBERS
1997-2001
Actual and projected

during 1997
10 m

during 1998
20 m

during 1999
30 m

during 2000
40 m

during 2001
50 m

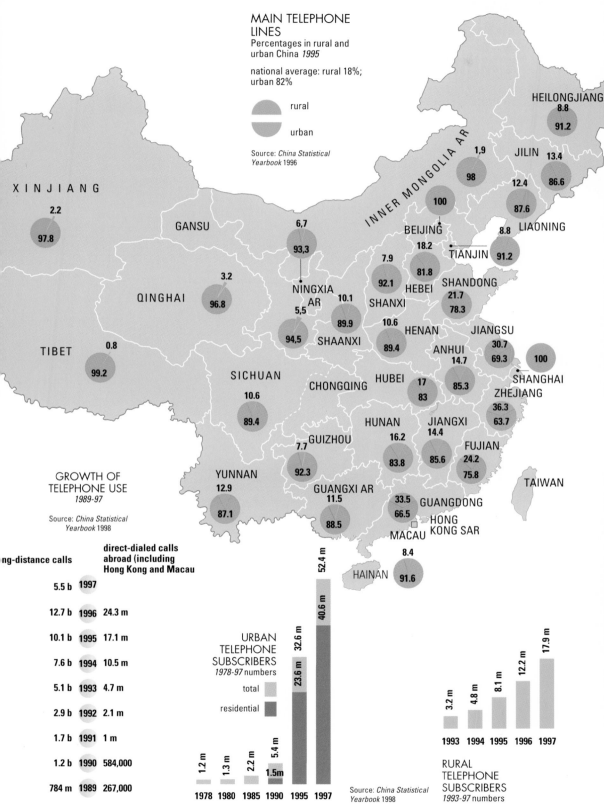

MAIN TELEPHONE LINES
Percentages in rural and urban China *1995*

national average: rural 18%; urban 82%

rural
urban

Source: *China Statistical Yearbook* 1996

XINJIANG 2.2 / 97.8
GANSU 6,7 / 93,3
QINGHAI 3.2 / 96.8
TIBET 0.8 / 99.2
INNER MONGOLIA AR 1,9 / 98
BEIJING 100
TIANJIN 18.2 / 81.8
NINGXIA AR 5,5 / 94,5
SHANXI 7.9 / 92.1
SHAANXI 10.1 / 89.9
HEBEI
SHANDONG 21.7 / 78.3
HENAN 10.6 / 89.4
JIANGSU 30.7 / 69.3
HEILONGJIANG 8.8 / 91.2
JILIN 13.4 / 86.6
LIAONING 12.4 / 87.6 · 8.8 / 91.2
SICHUAN 10.6 / 89.4
CHONGQING
HUBEI 17 / 83
ANHUI 14.7 / 85.3
SHANGHAI 100
ZHEJIANG 36.3 / 63.7
GUIZHOU 7.7 / 92.3
HUNAN 16.2 / 83.8
JIANGXI 14.4 / 85.6
FUJIAN 24.2 / 75.8
YUNNAN 12.9 / 87.1
GUANGXI AR 11.5 / 88.5
GUANGDONG 33.5 / 66.5
HONG KONG SAR
MACAU
TAIWAN
HAINAN 8.4 / 91.6

GROWTH OF TELEPHONE USE
1989-97

Source: *China Statistical Yearbook* 1998

long-distance calls | | direct-dialed calls abroad (including Hong Kong and Macau

long-distance calls	year	direct-dialed calls abroad
5.5 b	1997	
12.7 b	1996	24.3 m
10.1 b	1995	17.1 m
7.6 b	1994	10.5 m
5.1 b	1993	4.7 m
2.9 b	1992	2.1 m
1.7 b	1991	1 m
1.2 b	1990	584,000
784 m	1989	267,000

URBAN TELEPHONE SUBSCRIBERS
1978-97 numbers

total
residential

1978 1.2 m
1980 1.3 m
1985 2.2 m
1990 5.4 m / 1.5m
1995 32.6 m / 23.6 m
1997 52.4 m / 40.6 m

Source: *China Statistical Yearbook* 1998

RURAL TELEPHONE SUBSCRIBERS
1993-97 numbers

1993 3.2 m
1994 4.8 m
1995 8.1 m
1996 12.2 m
1997 17.9 m

THE CROWD THAT RECEIVES

The media are at the forefront of promoting the new consumerism as a spur to economic growth. By 2000, China's advertising revenue is expected to be the fourth largest in the world.

Television advertisments for generators have been replaced by advertising for hairsprays, tonics, and vitamins. Although China is the largest producer of toys, it has not yet targeted its own consumer market.

Star TV has gained an important foothold with permission to broadcast in southern China. Newpapers and magazines are an expanding market as they become more independent in their readership, and cater to changing lifestyles. Chinese-language editions of some international business and fashion magazines have been available since the late 1990s.

Robert Benewick and Stephanie Donald *The State of China Atlas* Copyright © Myriad Editions Limited

GROWTH OF MEDIA
1978-97
numbers

- 1978
- 1997

12	186	930
31	1,077	7,918
feature film studios	national/ provincial newspapers	magazines published

Southern Weekend, China's largest circulation weekly, has become known as the "hot little pepper", for its exposés.

Big Bird's Chinese cousin Da Niao was first shown on Shanghai TV in 1998. 130 episodes of Sesame Street (Zhima-Jie) have been recreated for a Chinese audience.

CONSUMER PRODUCTS ADVERTISED
Beijing *1996* percentages

Source: Wang, 1997

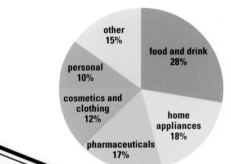

- food and drink 28%
- home appliances 18%
- pharmaceuticals 17%
- cosmetics and clothing 12%
- personal 10%
- other 15%

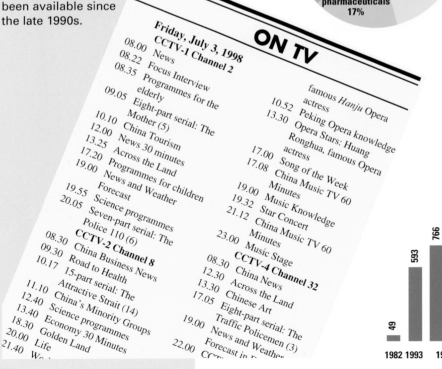

ON TV

Friday, July 3, 1998

CCTV-1 Channel 2
- 08.00 News
- 08.22 Focus Interview
- 08.35 Programmes for the elderly
- 09.05 Eight-part serial: The Mother (5)
- 10.10 China Tourism
- 12.00 News 30 minutes
- 13.25 Across the Land
- 17.20 Programmes for children
- 19.00 News and Weather Forecast
- 19.55 Science programmes
- 20.05 Seven-part serial: The Police 110 (6)

CCTV-2 Channel 8
- 08.30 China Business News
- 09.30 Road to Health
- 10.17 15-part serial: The Attractive Strait (14)
- 11.10 China's Minority Groups
- 12.40 Science programmes
- 13.40 Economy 30 Minutes
- 18.30 Golden Land
- 20.00 Life
- 21.40 W

- famous *Hanju* Opera actress
- 10.52 Peking Opera knowledge
- 13.30 Opera Stars: Huang Ronghua, famous Opera actress
- 17.00 Song of the Week
- 17.08 China Music TV 60 Minutes
- 19.00 Music Knowledge
- 19.32 Star Concert
- 21.12 China Music TV 60 Minutes
- 23.00 Music Stage

CCTV-4 Channel 32
- 08.30 China News
- 12.30 Across the Land
- 13.30 Chinese Art
- 17.05 Eight-part serial: The Traffic Policemen (3)
- 19.00 News and Weather Forecast in
- 22.00 CC

TV AND RADIO STATIONS
1982-96
numbers

- television
- radio

Source: Shoesmith, 1997; *China Statistical Yearbook* 1997

	1982	1993	1994	1995	1996	1997
television	49	593	837	880	923	
radio		766	1,117	1,202	1,244	1,363

By 2000, a national cable system is planned for 80 million households and 30% of China's television sets. In 1996, China Central Television's eight channels and 19 other provincial channels were being broadcast by satellite.

COLOR TVs
per 100 rural households
1996

national average: 27.3

- over 75
- 51-75
- 26-50
- 15-25
- below 15
- no data

Source: *China Statistical Yearbook* 1997

BLACK AND WHITE TVs
per 100 rural households
1996

national average: 65

more than 65

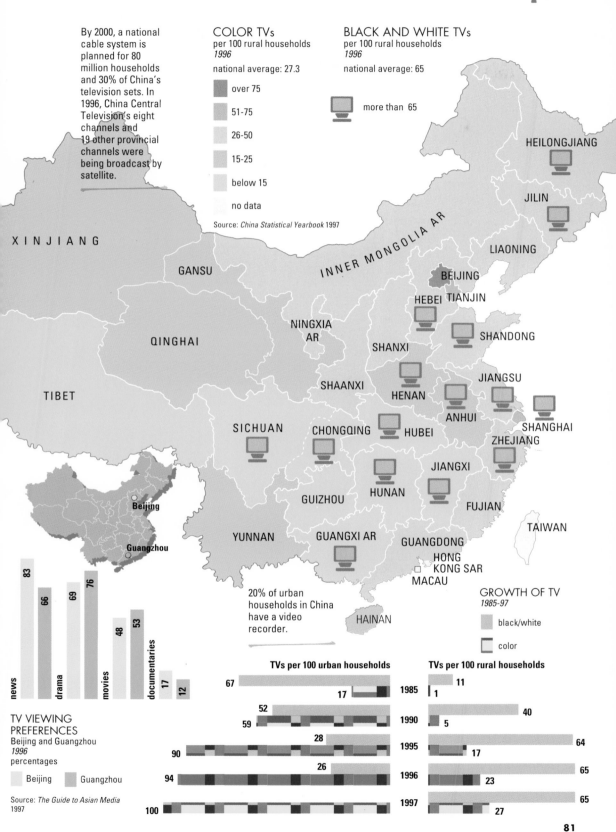

XINJIANG

GANSU

INNER MONGOLIA AR

HEILONGJIANG

JILIN

LIAONING

BEIJING

HEBEI TIANJIN

SHANDONG

NINGXIA AR

QINGHAI

SHANXI

SHAANXI

HENAN

JIANGSU

ANHUI

SHANGHAI

TIBET

ZHEJIANG

SICHUAN

CHONGQING HUBEI

JIANGXI

GUIZHOU HUNAN

FUJIAN

TAIWAN

YUNNAN

GUANGXI AR

GUANGDONG

HONG KONG SAR

MACAU

HAINAN

Beijing

Guangzhou

20% of urban households in China have a video recorder.

TV VIEWING PREFERENCES
Beijing and Guangzhou
1996
percentages

- Beijing
- Guangzhou

Source: *The Guide to Asian Media* 1997

news 83 / 66
drama 69 / 76
movies 48 / 53
documentaries 17 / 12

GROWTH OF TV
1985-97

- black/white
- color

TVs per 100 urban households

Year	color	black/white
1985	67	17
1990	52	59
1995	28	90
1996	26	94
1997	—	100

TVs per 100 rural households

Year	black/white	color
1985	11	1
1990	40	5
1995	64	17
1996	65	23
1997	65	27

Conservationists blame the all-time low in the world tiger population on the demand for traditional Chinese medicine. The South China tiger is the closest to extinction: in 1997, only 20 were remaining in the world.

Part Five
THE ENVIRONMENT

Robert Benewick and Stephanie Donald *The State of China Atlas* Copyright © Myriad Editions Limited

THE DAY WANES AND THE ROAD ENDS

One of China's foremost dilemmas is the conflict between environmental protection and short-term economic growth. Much of China's air pollution, including waste gas emission, has increased in line with industrial expansion.

However, China is ahead of other industrializing countries in facing up to environmental responsibilities and has set out a series of quotas to be achieved by 2000. High on the agenda, with the treatment of waste water and utilization of industrial solid waste, is the treatment of the industrial waste gas emissions shown on this map.

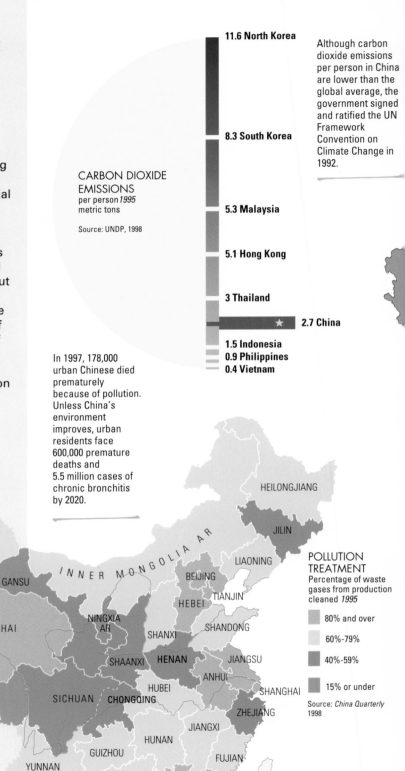

CARBON DIOXIDE EMISSIONS
per person *1995*
metric tons

Source: UNDP, 1998

11.6 North Korea

8.3 South Korea

5.3 Malaysia

5.1 Hong Kong

3 Thailand

★ 2.7 China

1.5 Indonesia
0.9 Philippines
0.4 Vietnam

Although carbon dioxide emissions per person in China are lower than the global average, the government signed and ratified the UN Framework Convention on Climate Change in 1992.

In 1997, 178,000 urban Chinese died prematurely because of pollution. Unless China's environment improves, urban residents face 600,000 premature deaths and 5.5 million cases of chronic bronchitis by 2020.

POLLUTION TREATMENT
Percentage of waste gases from production cleaned *1995*

- 80% and over
- 60%-79%
- 40%-59%
- 15% or under

Source: *China Quarterly* 1998

By 1997, China had closed down 57,000 small polluting factories.

Acid rain in China affects 40% of the country.

HEILONGJIANG
JILIN
XINJIANG
INNER MONGOLIA AR
LIAONING
GANSU
BEIJING
TIANJIN
HEBEI
QINGHAI
NINGXIA AR
SHANXI
SHANDONG
SHAANXI
HENAN
JIANGSU
TIBET
ANHUI
HUBEI
SHANGHAI
SICHUAN
CHONGQING
ZHEJIANG
JIANGXI
HUNAN
GUIZHOU
FUJIAN
YUNNAN
TAIWAN
GUANGXI AR
GUANGDONG
HAINAN

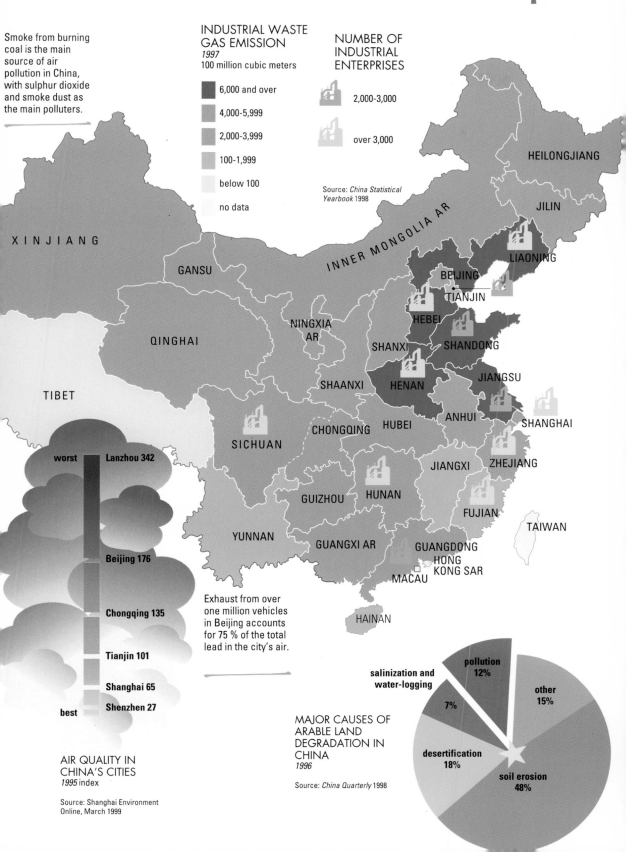

Smoke from burning coal is the main source of air pollution in China, with sulphur dioxide and smoke dust as the main polluters.

INDUSTRIAL WASTE GAS EMISSION
1997
100 million cubic meters

- 6,000 and over
- 4,000-5,999
- 2,000-3,999
- 100-1,999
- below 100
- no data

NUMBER OF INDUSTRIAL ENTERPRISES

- 2,000-3,000
- over 3,000

Source: *China Statistical Yearbook* 1998

XINJIANG

HEILONGJIANG

GANSU

INNER MONGOLIA AR

JILIN

LIAONING

BEIJING

TIANJIN

HEBEI

NINGXIA AR

SHANXI

SHANDONG

QINGHAI

SHAANXI

HENAN

JIANGSU

TIBET

SICHUAN

CHONGQING

HUBEI

ANHUI

SHANGHAI

ZHEJIANG

JIANGXI

GUIZHOU

HUNAN

FUJIAN

YUNNAN

GUANGXI AR

GUANGDONG

HONG KONG SAR

MACAU

TAIWAN

HAINAN

Exhaust from over one million vehicles in Beijing accounts for 75 % of the total lead in the city's air.

worst

Lanzhou 342

Beijing 176

Chongqing 135

Tianjin 101

Shanghai 65

Shenzhen 27

best

AIR QUALITY IN CHINA'S CITIES
1995 index

Source: Shanghai Environment Online, March 1999

MAJOR CAUSES OF ARABLE LAND DEGRADATION IN CHINA
1996

Source: *China Quarterly* 1998

pollution 12%

salinization and water-logging 7%

other 15%

desertification 18%

soil erosion 48%

Robert Benewick and Stephanie Donald *The State of China Atlas* Copyright © Myriad Editions Limited

NOT SINKING A WELL UNTIL ONE IS THIRSTY

The floods of 1998 reveal another side to China's economic growth. Deforestation leading to soil erosion, the encroachment by Chinese farmers on river beds, and the neglect of flood controls are some of the main causes of flooding.

Droughts are an even greater long-term problem. China's extensive dam-building program is designed, in part, to alleviate the worst effect of drought. The most spectacular of the dams, the Three Gorges, has proved to be the most controversial, raising fears of not only economic but also excessive environmental and human costs.

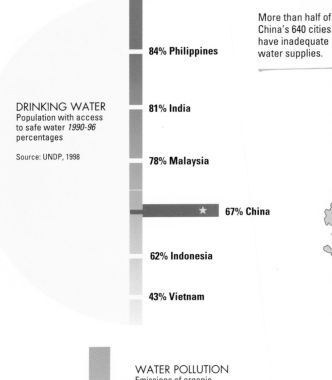

DRINKING WATER
Population with access to safe water *1990-96* percentages

Source: UNDP, 1998

89% Thailand

84% Philippines

81% India

78% Malaysia

★ 67% China

62% Indonesia

43% Vietnam

More than half of China's 640 cities have inadequate water supplies.

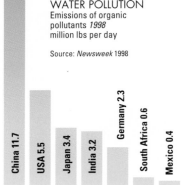

WATER POLLUTION
Emissions of organic pollutants *1998* million lbs per day

Source: *Newsweek* 1998

China 11.7 | USA 5.5 | Japan 3.4 | India 3.2 | Germany 2.3 | South Africa 0.6 | Mexico 0.4

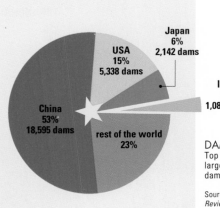

Japan
6%
2,142 dams

USA
15%
5,338 dams

India
3%
1,085 dams

China
53%
18,595 dams

rest of the world
23%

DAMS
Top four countries with largest share of world's dams *1997* percentages

Source: *Far Eastern Economic Review* 1997

CHINA

THREE GORGES DAM

Height of dam:	175 meters
length of reservoir:	600 km
total capacity:	39.3 billion m³
evacuation:	1.2 million people
submerging:	100 towns and villages in 44,000 hectares of land

Source: Seager, 1995; press reports

Yunyang
Fengjie
Wushan
Badong
HUBEI
Wanxian
Zhong Xian
Zigui
Yangtse River
Three Gorges Dam
Fengdu
new reservoir 600 kms (372 miles) long
Sandouping
Fuling
Gezhou Dam
Yichang
CHONGQING

☐ area flooded • large towns and cities affected

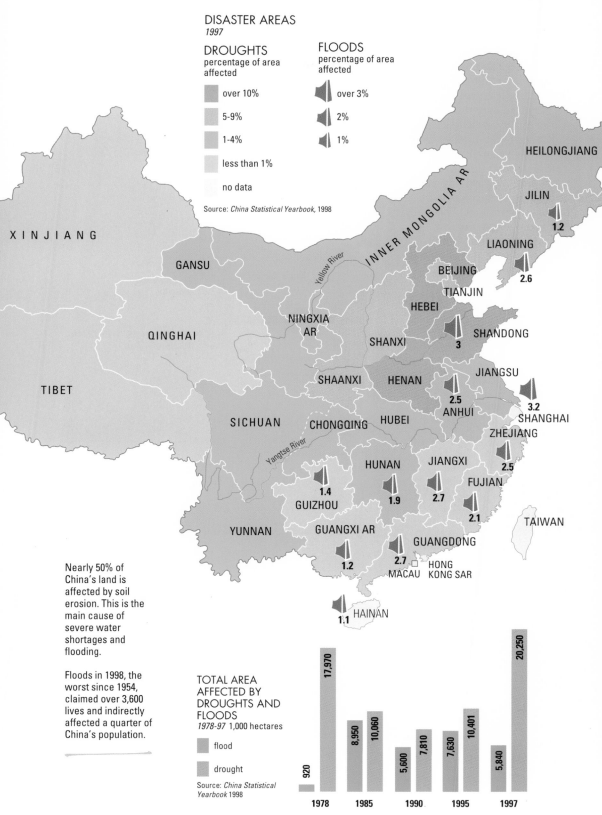

DISASTER AREAS
1997

DROUGHTS
percentage of area affected

- over 10%
- 5-9%
- 1-4%
- less than 1%
- no data

FLOODS
percentage of area affected

- over 3%
- 2%
- 1%

Source: *China Statistical Yearbook*, 1998

XINJIANG

HEILONGJIANG

JILIN
1.2

GANSU

INNER MONGOLIA AR

Yellow River

LIAONING
2.6

BEIJING

TIANJIN

HEBEI

SHANDONG

QINGHAI

NINGXIA AR

SHANXI

TIBET

SHAANXI

HENAN

JIANGSU

3.2

SHANGHAI

2.5

ANHUI

ZHEJIANG

2.5

SICHUAN

CHONGQING

HUBEI

Yangtse River

HUNAN

JIANGXI

FUJIAN

1.4

1.9

2.7

2.1

GUIZHOU

YUNNAN

GUANGXI AR

GUANGDONG

TAIWAN

1.2

2.7

MACAU

HONG KONG SAR

1.1 HAINAN

Nearly 50% of China's land is affected by soil erosion. This is the main cause of severe water shortages and flooding.

Floods in 1998, the worst since 1954, claimed over 3,600 lives and indirectly affected a quarter of China's population.

TOTAL AREA AFFECTED BY DROUGHTS AND FLOODS
1978-97 1,000 hectares

- flood
- drought

Source: *China Statistical Yearbook* 1998

	1978	1985	1990	1995	1997
flood	920	8,950	5,600	7,630	5,840
drought	17,970	10,060	7,810	10,401	20,250

WITH THE HIDE GONE, WHAT CAN THE HAIR ADHERE TO?

It is no surprise that a country as diverse as China has a wide variety of plant and animal life. Equally this very diversity is a threat to their existence. The number of endangered species as well as the extent of deforestation testifies to a huge and growing population struggling to survive and seeking to prosper. The state has taken steps towards damage limitation, if not preservation, but competing priorities and restricted resources hinder effective action.

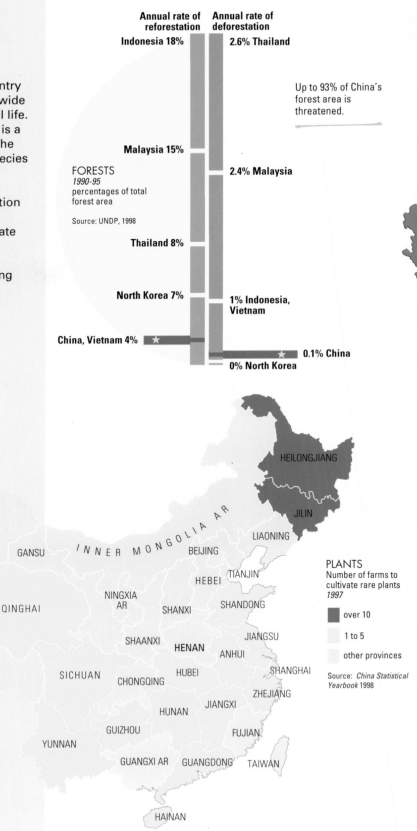

Annual rate of reforestation

Indonesia 18%

Malaysia 15%

FORESTS
1990-95
percentages of total forest area

Source: UNDP, 1998

Thailand 8%

North Korea 7%

China, Vietnam 4% ★

Annual rate of deforestation

2.6% Thailand

2.4% Malaysia

1% Indonesia, Vietnam

★ 0.1% China

0% North Korea

Up to 93% of China's forest area is threatened.

XINJIANG

GANSU

INNER MONGOLIA AR

QINGHAI

TIBET

NINGXIA AR

SHANXI

SHAANXI

HENAN

SICHUAN

CHONGQING

HUBEI

HUNAN

GUIZHOU

YUNNAN

GUANGXI AR

GUANGDONG

HAINAN

BEIJING

HEBEI

TIANJIN

SHANDONG

JIANGSU

ANHUI

SHANGHAI

ZHEJIANG

JIANGXI

FUJIAN

TAIWAN

HEILONGJIANG

JILIN

LIAONING

PLANTS
Number of farms to cultivate rare plants
1997

■ over 10

1 to 5

other provinces

Source: *China Statistical Yearbook* 1998

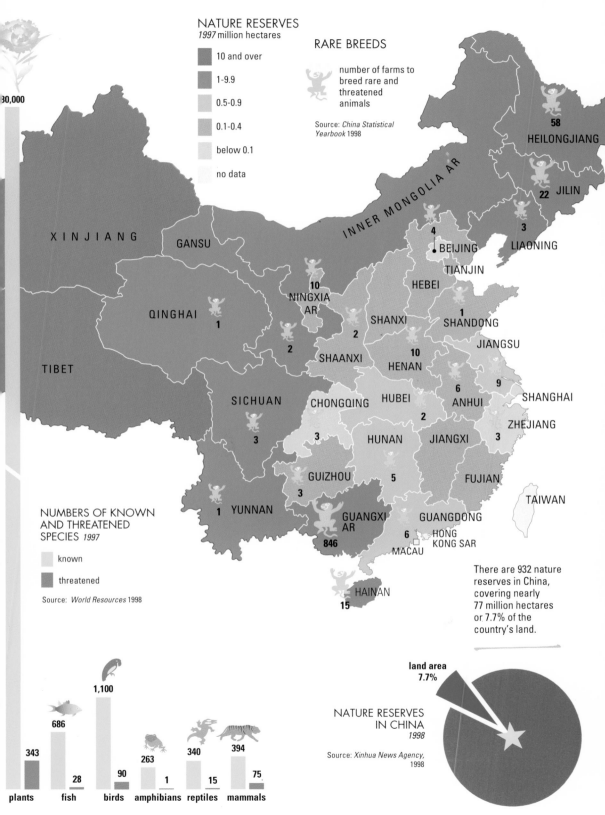

NATURE RESERVES
1997 million hectares

- 10 and over
- 1-9.9
- 0.5-0.9
- 0.1-0.4
- below 0.1
- no data

RARE BREEDS

number of farms to breed rare and threatened animals

Source: *China Statistical Yearbook* 1998

30,000

XINJIANG

GANSU

INNER MONGOLIA AR

HEILONGJIANG **58**

JILIN **22**

3 LIAONING

4 BEIJING

TIANJIN

HEBEI

1 SHANDONG

SHANXI **2**

JIANGSU

QINGHAI **1**

NINGXIA AR **10**

SHAANXI **2**

HENAN **10**

6 ANHUI **9**

SHANGHAI

TIBET

SICHUAN

CHONGQING

HUBEI **2**

ZHEJIANG **3**

3 HUNAN

JIANGXI

GUIZHOU **3**

5

FUJIAN

YUNNAN **1**

GUANGXI AR **846**

GUANGDONG

6 HONG KONG SAR

MACAU

TAIWAN

HAINAN **15**

NUMBERS OF KNOWN AND THREATENED SPECIES *1997*

- known
- threatened

Source: *World Resources* 1998

There are 932 nature reserves in China, covering nearly 77 million hectares or 7.7% of the country's land.

land area 7.7%

NATURE RESERVES IN CHINA
1998

Source: *Xinhua News Agency,* 1998

plants	fish	birds	amphibians	reptiles	mammals
343	686	1,100	263	340	394
28	90	1	15	75	

In 1994 China
drafted an agenda for
the twenty first century,
China Agenda 21,
implemented a plan on
priority projects, and
issued a national report
on sustainable
development. By 1998,
25 provinces,
autonomous regions,
and municipalities had
adopted the Agenda.

CHINA IN TRANSITION

THE TREE PREFERS CALM BUT THE WIND DOES NOT STOP

There are many ways to measure and judge China's development. As the fastest-growing economy, it may overtake the USA. As the largest population, it may be dwarfed by India. China has a poor record on corruption but in gender empowerment it ranks higher than many other Asian countries. It has invested in environmental programs and sustainable development. Ultimately, however, China's position in the world is not as important as its internal development.

The market economy has affected every aspect of life in China. The United Nations' Human Development Index measures income, longevity, and education to compare the quality of life between countries. In 1995, the same index was used to compare China's development by province. The breadth of difference between Shanghai (with the same score as Argentina) and Tibet (with the same score as Nigeria) reflects a telling profile of modern China and the impossibility of even development.

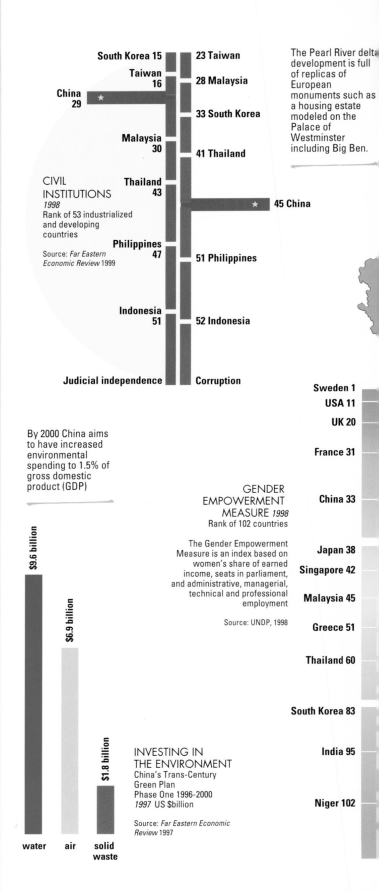

South Korea 15
Taiwan 16
China 29
Malaysia 30
Thailand 43
Philippines 47
Indonesia 51

Judicial independence

CIVIL INSTITUTIONS
1998
Rank of 53 industrialized and developing countries

Source: Far Eastern Economic Review 1999

23 Taiwan
28 Malaysia
33 South Korea
41 Thailand
45 China
51 Philippines
52 Indonesia

Corruption

The Pearl River delta development is full of replicas of European monuments such as a housing estate modeled on the Palace of Westminster including Big Ben.

By 2000 China aims to have increased environmental spending to 1.5% of gross domestic product (GDP)

$9.6 billion
$6.9 billion
$1.8 billion
water air solid waste

INVESTING IN THE ENVIRONMENT
China's Trans-Century Green Plan
Phase One 1996-2000
1997 US $billion

Source: Far Eastern Economic Review 1997

GENDER EMPOWERMENT MEASURE 1998
Rank of 102 countries

The Gender Empowerment Measure is an index based on women's share of earned income, seats in parliament, and administrative, managerial, technical and professional employment

Source: UNDP, 1998

Sweden 1
USA 11
UK 20
France 31
China 33
Japan 38
Singapore 42
Malaysia 45
Greece 51
Thailand 60
South Korea 83
India 95
Niger 102

In 1998, in a speech marking 20 years of economic reforms, President Jiang Zemin pledged to smash opposition to the Communist Party and vowed that China would never adopt Western-style democracy.

RELATIVE HUMAN DEVELOPMENT
1995 index

The Human Development Index is based on three key components: longevity, education, and income

- 800 or over
- 700-799 *medium*
- 600-699
- 500-599
- under 400 *very low*
- no data

Source: *China Human Development Report* 1997

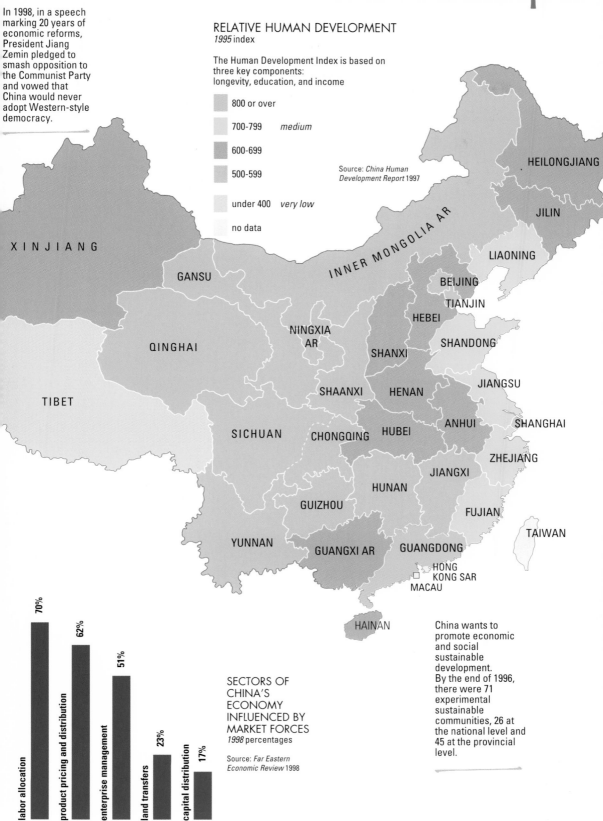

XINJIANG

GANSU

INNER MONGOLIA AR

HEILONGJIANG

JILIN

LIAONING

BEIJING

TIANJIN

HEBEI

SHANDONG

NINGXIA AR

SHANXI

QINGHAI

TIBET

SHAANXI

HENAN

JIANGSU

SICHUAN

CHONGQING

HUBEI

ANHUI

SHANGHAI

ZHEJIANG

JIANGXI

HUNAN

GUIZHOU

FUJIAN

TAIWAN

YUNNAN

GUANGXI AR

GUANGDONG

HONG KONG SAR

MACAU

HAINAN

SECTORS OF CHINA'S ECONOMY INFLUENCED BY MARKET FORCES
1998 percentages

Source: *Far Eastern Economic Review* 1998

- **labor allocation** 70%
- **product pricing and distribution** 62%
- **enterprise management** 51%
- **land transfers** 23%
- **capital distribution** 17%

China wants to promote economic and social sustainable development. By the end of 1996, there were 71 experimental sustainable communities, 26 at the national level and 45 at the provincial level.

PROVINCE TABLES

Provinces	1 Land area 1999 km²	2 Population 1997 1,000s	3 Population by age 1997 under-15s	15 to 64-year-olds 1,000s	over 64
Beijing	16,808	12,850	2,120	9,598	1,13
Tianjin	11,300	9,678	1,934	6,929	81
Hebei	187,700	66,283	16,918	44,959	4,40
Shanxi	156,000	31,908	8,675	21,245	1,98
Inner Mongolia	1,200,000	23,611	5,832	16,570	1,20
Liaoning	146,000	42,039	7,984	30,771	3,28
Jilin	187,400	26,697	5,574	19,469	1,65
Heilongjiang	469,000	38,108	8,342	28,009	1,75
Shanghai	6,340	14,913	2,324	10,766	1,82
Jiangsu	102,600	72,562	15,593	50,555	6,41
Zhejiang	101,800	45,051	8,704	32,177	4,17
Anhui	140,000	62,199	15,576	42,407	4,21
Fujian	121,700	33,321	9,431	21,513	2,37
Jiangxi	166,600	42,158	11,394	28,288	2,47
Shandong	156,700	89,178	20,748	61,418	7,01
Henan	167,000	93,916	25,098	62,400	6,41
Hubei	185,900	59,677	16,292	39,846	3,54
Hunan	212,000	65,670	16,158	44,716	4,79
Guangdong	178,000	71,580	20,509	45,850	5,22
Guangxi	236,660	47,115	13,454	30,071	3,59
Hainan	33,940	7,560	2,361	4,715	48
Sichuan	570,000	85,642	19,963	58,855	6,82
Chongqing	–	30,904	7,234	21,142	2,52
Guizhou	174,000	36,631	10,722	23,860	2,04
Yunnan	394,000	41,589	11,338	27,678	2,57
Tibet	1,230,000	2,479	825	1,519	13
Shaanxi	205,600	36,269	10,020	24,127	2,12
Gansu	454,000	25,340	6,964	17,166	1,20
Qinghai	720,000	5,035	1,446	3,359	23
Ningxia	66,400	5,384	1,590	3,563	23
Xinjiang	1,600,000	17,453	5,280	11,377	79

Sources: col 1: Goddard, 1997; cols 2 and 3: *China Statistical Yearbook* 1998

Population by gender 1997		Nationality 1996		Human Development Index 1996	Provinces
4		**5**		**6**	
male	female	Han	other nationality	rank	
1,000s					
6,427	6,423	124,042	4,967	2	Beijing
4,842	4,835	94,775	2,265	3	Tianjin
33,565	32,719	637,507	24,653	12	Hebei
16,385	15,523	315,827	661	14	Shanxi
12,117	11,494	180,181	54,736	22	Inner Mongolia
21,274	20,765	345,369	75,996	7	Liaoning
13,596	13,101	237,621	29,264	13	Jilin
19,426	18,682	358,414	22,527	10	Heilongjiang
7,337	7,576	145,046	771	1	Shanghai
36,143	36,420	725,269	2,065	6	Jiangsu
22,821	22,230	441,517	3,154	5	Zhejiang
31,963	30,236	614,178	4,257	19	Anhui
16,875	16,446	326,509	6,376	8	Fujian
21,680	20,478	415,649	1,695	23	Jiangxi
44,886	44,292	891,902	4,350	9	Shandong
48,048	45,868	925,232	10,207	16	Henan
30,655	29,023	569,818	23,764	17	Hubei
33,701	31,969	569,026	89,628	20	Hunan
36,482	35,098	700,545	4,618	4	Guangdong
24,646	22,468	267,398	199,445	18	Guangxi
3,927	3,633	59,080	15,170	11	Hainan
43,417	42,225	1,106,756	56,588	21	Sichuan
15,748	15,156	–	–	–	Chongqing
19,119	17,512	227,876	132,543	29	Guizhou
21,087	20,501	262,054	147,452	26	Yunnan
1,207	1,272	825	23,822	30	Tibet
18,633	17,635	358,525	2,410	25	Shaanxi
12,932	12,408	226,761	23,418	27	Gansu
2,536	2,499	24,223	25,173	28	Qinghai
2,730	2,653	34,839	17,651	24	Ningxia
8,875	8,578	67,813	102,754	15	Xinjiang

ces: **col 4:** *China Statistical Yearbook* 1998; **col 5:** *China Population Statistics Yearbook* 1997; **col 6:** *China Human Development Report* 1997

PROVINCE TABLES

Provinces	7 Population by residence 1996 1,000s		8 Number employed 1997 10,000s	9 Share of employment 1997 percentages	
	rural	urban		men	women
Beijing	3,228	9,731	660.8	55.8	44.2
Tianjin	3,300	6,458	491.6	55.7	44.3
Hebei	53,656	13,023	3,415	54.3	45.7
Shanxi	22,480	9,394	1,483.2	55.5	44.5
Inner Mongolia	15,066	8,594	1,050.3	55.3	44.7
Liaoning	19,908	22,485	2,063.3	54.2	45.8
Jilin	14,145	12,704	1,237.3	54.6	45.4
Heilongjiang	18,020	20,318	1,658.6	56.5	43.5
Shanghai	2,461	12,197	770.2	53.6	46.4
Jiangsu	51,724	21,471	3,745.5	51.8	48.2
Zhejiang	30,083	14,660	2,700.3	57.3	42.7
Anhui	47,264	15,463	3,321.7	53.6	46.4
Fujian	26,131	7,403	1,613.4	54.7	45.3
Jiangxi	32,363	9,721	2,077.7	53.7	46.3
Shandong	58,374	31,809	4,707	52.9	47.1
Henan	78,602	15,670	5,017	52.5	47.5
Hubei	39,618	20,173	2,708.7	52.9	47.1
Hunan	50,378	15,839	3,590.7	53.5	46.5
Guangdong	49,226	21,918	3,784.3	52.7	47.3
Guangxi	38,124	8,931	2,452.4	52.7	47.3
Hainan	5,667	1,832	330.9	53.1	46.9
Sichuan	84,100	33,204	4,617.6	52.3	47.7
Chongqing	–	–	1,689.9	52.6	47.4
Guizhou	25,753	10,590	1,927.1	53.5	46.5
Yunnan	34,269	7,059	2,247.6	52.1	47.9
Tibet	1,897	590	120.3	48.6	51.4
Shaanxi	26,852	9,551	1,811.9	54.2	45.8
Gansu	20,084	5,173	1185.9	53	47
Qinghai	3,599	1,384	235.4	52.6	47.4
Ningxia	3,771	1,543	260.4	53	47
Xinjiang	10,754	6,453	690.7	54.1	45.9

Sources: **col 7**: *China Population Statistics Yearbook 1997*; **cols 8 and 9**: *China Statistical Yearbook 1998*

	10 Employment by sector 1997 percentages		11 Unemployed 1996 10,000s	Provinces
primary	secondary	tertiary		
10.7	38.2	51.1	7.15	Beijing
16.5	45.9	37.6	12.45	Tianjin
47.8	27.5	24.6	26.92	Hebei
43	28.6	28.4	19.31	Shanxi
51.9	20.3	27.9	29.55	Inner Mongolia
32.2	35.2	32.7	72.96	Liaoning
44.6	25.5	29.9	26.68	Jilin
39.4	30.8	29.8	51.50	Heilongjiang
10	45.8	44.2	29.82	Shanghai
41.6	32.5	25.8	45.82	Jiangsu
41.3	30.9	27.8	30.88	Zhejiang
59.6	16.7	23.7	35.77	Anhui
48.5	24.7	26.8	24.05	Fujian
54	17.8	28.2	29.29	Jiangxi
53.3	24.6	22.1	63.56	Shandong
58.1	20.1	21.8	48.68	Henan
48.6	21.8	29.6	54.68	Hubei
58.9	16.2	24.9	56	Hunan
40.4	27.7	32	71.07	Guangdong
65.6	11.5	22.9	31.68	Guangxi
61.2	11.6	27.3	7.15	Hainan
62.2	15.5	22.3	74.01	Sichuan
57.2	17.2	25.6	–	Chongqing
72.1	10	18	29.34	Guizhou
74.7	9.8	15.6	19.90	Yunnan
76	4.9	19	–	Tibet
58.1	18.7	23.2	37.78	Shaanxi
58.1	16.6	25.3	25.74	Gansu
60	16.9	23.1	8.77	Qinghai
58.1	18.9	23	7.14	Ningxia
56.8	17.1	26.2	22.52	Xinjiang

ces: col 10: *China Statistical Yearbook* 1998; col 11: *China Labor Statistical Yearbook* 1997

PROVINCE TABLES

Provinces	12 Gross Domestic Product (GDP) 1997 100 million yuan	13 GDP per person 1997 yuan	14 GDP by sector 1997 100 million yuan primary	secondary	tertiary
Beijing	1,810.09	16,735	84.85	738.56	986.6
Tianjin	1,240.40	13,796	74.55	643.88	521.9
Hebei	3,953.78	6,079	761.76	1,934.38	1,257.6
Shanxi	1,480.13	4,736	191.84	789.45	498.8
Inner Mongolia	1,094.52	4,691	322.52	445.50	326.5
Liaoning	3,490.06	8,525	485.38	1,743.87	1,260.8
Jilin	1,446.91	5,504	368.16	575.43	503.3
Heilongjiang	2,708.46	7,243	484.81	1,449.25	774.4
Shanghai	3,360.21	25,750	75.80	1,754.39	1,530.0
Jiangsu	6,680.34	9,344	1,008.41	3,411.86	2,260.0
Zhejiang	4,638.24	10,515	637.48	2,509.56	1,491.2
Anhui	2,669.95	4,390	732.37	1,260.90	676.6
Fujian	3,000.36	9,258	576.63	1,293.50	1,130.2
Jiangxi	1,715.18	4,155	475.18	658.25	581.7
Shandong	6,650.02	7,590	1,195	3,185.05	2,269.9
Henan	4,079.26	4,430	1,008.55	1,920.05	1,150.6
Hubei	3,450.24	5,899	767.92	1,606.98	1,075.3
Hunan	2,993	4,643	855.75	1,166.97	970.2
Guangdong	7,315.51	10,428	986.82	3,647.82	2,680.8
Guangxi	2,015.20	4,356	631.62	759.54	624.0
Hainan	409.86	5,698	151.28	82.68	175.9
Sichuan	3,320.11	4,029	919.28	1,385.38	1,015.4
Chongqing	1,350.10	4,452	304.51	563.40	482.1
Guizhou	792.98	2,215	271.83	293.47	227.6
Yunnan	1,644.23	4,042	391.48	750.01	502.7
Tibet	76.98	3,194	29.18	16.95	30.8
Shaanxi	1,326.04	3,707	271.52	555.86	498.6
Gansu	781.34	3,137	189.79	343.40	248.1
Qinghai	202.05	4,066	40.65	78.80	82.6
Ningxia	210.92	4,025	44.82	87.65	78.4
Xinjiang	1,050.14	5,904	279.73	413.29	357.1

Sources: cols **12** to **14**: *China Statistical Yearbook* 1998

15 Trade 1997 US $10,000	16 Imports and exports 1997 US $10,000		17 Foreign Direct Investment and other investments 1997 US $10,000	Provinces
	Exports	imports		
1,562,083	583,399	978,684	159,286	Beijing
1,069,713	518,061	551,652	251,135	Tianjin
398,054	263,833	134,221	110,308	Hebei
242,161	196,974	45,187	26,893	Shanxi
96,889	58,894	37,995	7,325	Inner Mongolia
1,477,162	811,031	666,131	236,635	Liaoning
247,008	142,938	104,070	40,227	Jilin
440,234	332,029	108,205	73,485	Heilongjiang
3,036,566	1,476,727	1,559,839	422,536	Shanghai
2,537,042	1,443,307	1,093,735	543,511	Jiangsu
1,625,262	1,074,580	550,682	150,345	Zhejiang
263,651	155,772	107,879	43,443	Anhui
1,925,536	1,101,443	824,093	419,710	Fujian
122,816	89,243	33,573	48,103	Jiangxi
1,995,909	1,171,708	824,201	277,556	Shandong
239,450	143,561	95,889	69,204	Henan
320,763	169,296	151,467	84,866	Hubei
205,347	147,135	58,212	91,702	Hunan
13,257,932	7,594,969	5,662,963	1,263,495	Guangdong
248,371	166,642	81,729	88,579	Guangxi
192,517	79,209	113,308	70,554	Hainan
362,088	186,606	175,482	24,846	Sichuan
–	–	–	41,802	Chongqing
71,471	47,324	24,147	4,977	Guizhou
162,602	102,284	60,318	16,566	Yunnan
14,443	2,276	12,167	–	Tibet
170,822	102,909	67,913	62,816	Shaanxi
51,563	32,718	18,845	4,144	Gansu
15,138	12,406	2,732	247	Qinghai
27,039	21,565	5,474	671	Ningxia
126,113	40,825	85,288	2,472	Xinjiang

rces: cols 15 to 17: *China Statistical Yearbook* 1998

PROVINCE TABLES

Provinces	18 Telephones 1997 per 100 urban households	19 Computers 1997 per 100 urban households	20 Color TVs 1997 per 100 urban households	21 Air conditioners 1997 per 100 urban households	22 Refrigerators 1? per 100 urban households
Beijing	1.20	12.20	123.80	27.20	104.20
Tianjin	1.20	5	110.60	25.20	97
Hebei	1.28	1.57	100.11	13.66	81.45
Shanxi	0.91	1.35	99.54	2.35	66.46
Inner Mongolia	2.09	1.13	93.34	0.30	53.86
Liaoning	1.25	1.45	98.21	0.57	72.66
Jilin	0.76	0.84	92.46	–	54.87
Heilongjiang	1.43	0.86	91.23	0.13	52.56
Shanghai	2.40	8.60	118.60	62.20	101.60
Jiangsu	1.79	2.22	101.11	22.89	77.68
Zhejiang	2.45	3.08	111.01	35.22	97.42
Anhui	1.06	1.05	90.92	14.95	75.37
Fujian	4.16	2.24	109.44	20.24	84.48
Jiangxi	1.53	1.78	91.53	12.37	73.22
Shandong	1.32	1.77	100.67	11.35	82.24
Henan	1.15	1.09	95.84	18.86	67.08
Hubei	2.25	1.36	93.96	20.68	81.70
Hunan	2	2.68	95.14	18.13	81.38
Guangdong	7.30	9.05	119.13	63.68	78.16
Guangxi	1	1.58	98.63	10.21	73.96
Hainan	0.90	1.60	101.40	6.60	48.60
Sichuan	0.59	1.80	104.87	5.12	78.38
Chongqing	2	4	107	59.33	98.67
Guizhou	–	1.20	100.90	0.87	71.92
Yunnan	1.76	1.58	101.33	0.07	61.04
Tibet	–	–	–	–	–
Shaanxi	0.18	0.91	102.02	14.81	67.51
Gansu	0.58	2.20	99.52	–	58.26
Qinghai	8.44	1.78	100.89	0.22	57.33
Ningxia	–	1.06	101.83	0.17	64.54
Xinjiang	–	0.99	97.74	2.41	74.11

Sources: cols 18 to 22: *China Statistical Yearbook* 1998

23 Washing machines 1997 per 100 urban households	24 Cars 1997 per 100 urban households	25 Bicycles 1997 per 100 urban households	26 Motorcycles 1997 per 100 urban households	27 Soft beds 1997 per 100 urban households	Provinces
100.60	0.80	209.40	4.20	65.80	Beijing
94.40	–	225.80	10.60	40.60	Tianjin
91.71	0.19	234.49	21.21	41.54	Hebei
93.07	0.23	203.78	13.54	27.13	Shanxi
83.02	0.90	203.63	14.26	25.85	Inner Mongolia
86.77	0.16	164.01	4.54	40.51	Liaoning
88.87	0.17	173.06	2.88	36.56	Jilin
82.22	–	149.71	5.01	37.34	Heilongjiang
86.80	–	125.40	1.20	28.20	Shanghai
94.98	–	225.32	15.57	29.73	Jiangsu
87.30	0.19	220.63	8.68	23.77	Zhejiang
86.23	0.14	162.20	8.44	17.52	Anhui
92.56	0.16	175.44	22.88	30.64	Fujian
81.69	0.08	165.08	7.88	40.93	Jiangxi
86.51	0.05	228.65	20.61	60.57	Shandong
87.31	0.03	219.13	12.06	44.33	Henan
90.27	0.15	153.03	4.43	38.15	Hubei
94.03	–	137.20	7.93	34.44	Hunan
99.16	0.30	212.26	37.23	65.19	Guangdong
87.56	0.18	216.11	24.27	35.71	Guangxi
75.50	–	111	25.50	36.70	Hainan
92.68	0.44	112.99	6.20	50.45	Sichuan
89.67	–	10.33	0.67	21.33	Chongqing
92.74	–	34.99	7.04	30.75	Guizhou
92.38	–	180.27	9.71	41.80	Yunnan
–	–	–	–	–	Tibet
92.23	–	173.85	4.79	55.81	Shaanxi
85.38	0.17	176.10	5.06	63.10	Gansu
99.56	–	152	8.44	51.33	Qinghai
88.28	0.17	195.48	8.82	54.81	Ningxia
88.12	0.99	169.93	8.54	88.43	Xinjiang

ırces: cols 23 to 27: *China Statistical Yearbook* 1998

CHINA IN THE WORLD

Countries	1 Land area 1999 1,000 km²	2 Population 1996 1,000s	3 Life expectancy at birth 1996 years	4 Infant mortality rate 1996 per 1,000 live births
Argentina	2,736.7	35,220	73	22
Australia	7,682.3	18,312	78	6
Brazil	8,456.5	161,365	67	36
Bulgaria	110.6	8,356	71	16
Burma	657.6	45,883	60	80
Canada	9,221	29,964	79	6
China	**9,326.4**	**1,215,414**	**70**	**33**
Czech Republic	77.3	10,315	74	6
Egypt	995.5	59,272	65	53
France	550.1	58,375	78	5
Germany	349.3	81,912	76	5
Hong Kong	**1**	**6,311**	**79**	**4**
India	2,973.2	945,121	63	65
Indonesia	1,811.6	197,055	65	49
Israel	20.6	5,692	77	6
Italy	294.1	57,380	78	6
Japan	376.5	125,761	80	4
Korea (South)	98.7	45,545	72	9
Malaysia	328.6	20,565	72	11
Mexico	1,908.7	93,182	72	32
Nigeria	910.8	114,568	53	78
Norway	306.8	4,381	78	4
Pakistan	770.9	133,510	63	88
Philippines	298.2	71,899	66	37
Poland	304.4	38,618	72	12
Romania	230.3	22,608	69	22
Russia	16,888.5	147,739	66	17
Singapore	0.6	3,044	76	4
South Africa	1,221	37,643	65	49
Spain	499.4	39,260	77	5
Sweden	411.6	8,843	79	4
Tanzania	883.6	30,494	50	86
Thailand	510.9	60,003	69	34
Turkey	769.6	62,697	69	42
United Kingdom	241.6	58,782	77	6
USA	9,159.1	265,284	77	7

Sources: cols 1 to 4: *World Bank Atlas,* 1998

5 Adult literacy 1995 percentages	6 Access to safe water 1990-1996 percentage of population	7 Women in the labor force 1996 percentage of total	8 Human Development Index 1995 rank of 174 countries	Countries
96	71	31	36	Argentina
100	100	43	15	Australia
83	76	35	62	Brazil
98	100	48	67	Bulgaria
83	60	43	131	Burma
97	100	45	1	Canada
82	**67**	**45**	**106**	**China**
–	100	47	39	Czech Republic
51	87	29	112	Egypt
–	100	44	2	France
–	100	42	19	Germany
–	**–**	**37**	**25**	**Hong Kong**
52	81	32	139	India
84	62	40	96	Indonesia
95	100	40	22	Israel
98	100	38	21	Italy
–	97	41	8	Japan
98	93	41	30	Korea (South)
84	78	37	60	Malaysia
90	83	31	49	Mexico
57	50	36	142	Nigeria
–	100	46	3	Norway
38	74	27	138	Pakistan
95	84	37	98	Philippines
–	100	46	52	Poland
98	100	44	74	Romania
99	100	49	72	Russia
91	100	38	28	Singapore
82	99	37	89	South Africa
97	100	36	11	Spain
–	100	48	10	Sweden
68	38	49	150	Tanzania
94	89	46	59	Thailand
82	49	36	69	Turkey
–	100	43	14	United Kingdom
99	100	46	4	USA

rces: cols 5 and 6: Unicef, 1998: col 7: *World Bank Atlas,* 1998; col 8: *Human Development Report* 1998

CHINA IN THE WORLD

Countries	9 Gross National Product (GNP) 1996 US$ millions	10 GNP per person 1996 US$	11 Trade in goods and services 1996 percentage of GDP	12 Foreign Direct Investment 1996 percentage of GDP	13 International tourism 1996 receipts US$ milli
Argentina	295,131	8,380	14	1.5	4,572
Australia	367,802	20,090	34	1.6	8,703
Brazil	709,591	4,400	10.2	1.3	2,469
Bulgaria	9,924	1,190	23.8	1.2	450
Burma	–	–	–	–	90
Canada	569,899	19,020	58.5	1.1	8,868
China	**906,079**	**750**	**7.1**	**4.9**	**10,200**
Czech Republic	48,861	4,740	46.3	2.6	4,075
Egypt	64,275	1,080	14.8	0.9	3,200
France	1,533,619	26,270	45.4	1.4	28,357
Germany	2,364,632	28,870	55.1	-0.1	16,496
Hong Kong	**153,288**	**24,290**	**247.6**	**–**	**10,836**
India	357,759	380	4.5	0.7	3,027
Indonesia	213,384	1,080	13.6	3.5	6,087
Israel	90,310	15,870	47.5	1.7	2,800
Italy	1,140,484	19,880	39.6	0.3	28,673
Japan	5,149,185	40,940	26.1	0	4,078
Korea (South)	483,130	10,610	46.7	0.5	5,430
Malaysia	89,800	4,370	70.2	4.5	3,926
Mexico	341,718	3,670	26.1	2.3	6,934
Nigeria	27,599	240	21.5	4.3	85
Norway	151,198	34,510	80.3	2.5	2,404
Pakistan	63,567	480	10	1.1	146
Philippines	83,298	1,160	21.3	1.7	2,701
Poland	124,682	3,230	26.5	3.3	8,400
Romania	36,191	1,600	16.8	0.7	20
Russia	356,030	2,410	19.8	0.6	5,542
Singapore	92,987	30,550	316	10	7,916
South Africa	132,455	3,520	20.7	0.1	1,995
Spain	563,249	14,350	36.8	1.1	27,414
Sweden	227,315	25,710	87.2	2.2	3,683
Tanzania	5,174	170	–	2.6	322
Thailand	177,476	2,960	31.3	1.3	8,664
Turkey	177,530	2,830	17.5	0.4	5,962
United Kingdom	1,152,136	19,600	46.3	2.8	19,296
United States	7,433,517	28,020	19.4	1	64,373

Sources: cols 9 to 13: *World Bank Atlas*, 1998

14 Telephone mainlines 1996 per 1,000 people	15 Personal computers 1996 per 1,000 people	16 Water use 1980-96 annual per person meter^3	17 Energy use 1995 per person kg	18 Carbon dioxide emissions 1995 metric tonnes per person	Countries
174	24.6	1,043	1,525	3.7	Argentina
519	311.3	933	5,215	16	Australia
96	18.4	246	772	1.6	Brazil
313	295.2	1,574	2,724	6.7	Bulgaria
4	–	101	50	0.2	Burma
602	192.5	1,602	7,879	14.7	Canada
45	**3**	**461**	**707**	**2.7**	**China**
273	53.2	266	3,776	10.8	Czech Republic
50	5.8	921	596	1.6	Egypt
564	150.7	665	4,150	5.8	France
538	233.2	580	4,156	10.2	Germany
547	**150.5**	**–**	**2,212**	**5**	**Hong Kong**
15	1.5	612	260	1	India
21	4.8	96	442	1.5	Indonesia
446	117.6	407	3,003	8.4	Israel
440	92.3	986	2,821	7.2	Italy
489	128	735	3,964	9	Japan
430	131.7	632	3,225	8.3	Korea (South)
183	42.8	768	1,655	5.3	Malaysia
95	29	915	1,456	3.9	Mexico
4	4.1	41	165	0.8	Nigeria
555	273	488	5,439	16.6	Norway
18	1.2	1,269	243	0.7	Pakistan
25	9.3	686	307	0.9	Philippines
169	36.2	321	2,448	8.8	Poland
140	5.3	1,139	1,941	5.3	Romania
175	23.7	521	4,079	12.3	Russia
513	216.8	84	7,162	21.3	Singapore
100	37.7	359	2,405	8.3	South Africa
392	94.2	781	2,639	5.9	Spain
682	214.9	340	5,736	5	Sweden
3	–	40	32	0.1	Tanzania
70	16.7	602	878	2.9	Thailand
224	13.8	544	1,009	2.7	Turkey
528	192.6	204	3,786	9.3	United Kingdom
640	362.4	1,839	7,905	20.8	USA

urces: cols 14 to 18: *World Bank Atlas, 1998*

COMMENTARY ON THE MAPS

1 Population

We begin the atlas with people because the numbers are so staggering that everything else about China must follow and so must all our maps. Although the rate of population growth may be decreasing in China, and although the population in China and Asia looks set to remain a stable proportion of the world's population over the next 25 years, the actual population is still large and is growing.

From the weight of sheer numbers, policy implications flow. In 2020 there are expected to be 230 million people in China over 60 years of age (**Map 27**). On the one hand this is a measure of the improvements in lifestyle, medicine and nutrition. On the other hand, it presents the problem of how China is going to deal with the pensions, housing and health care needed on such a massive scale. And, to complete the picture, the declining birth rate means there will be a smaller work force to support a larger elderly population.

Uneven distribution of the population is a reflection of economic growth. This exposes a developmental conundrum. In so far as China's leaders have pursued "a highly interventionist and aggressive policy" (Conway, 1997) of population control as an imperative to modernization, it conflicts with the notion that it is China's cheap and plentiful labor which makes it competitive in a global market.

Sources: Gordon Conway, *The Double Green Revolution*, London: Penguin Books, 1997

2 Urbanization

At the beginning of the reform period in 1978, 82 percent of China's population was classified as rural. Today, the proportion of the population that is rural is down to 70 percent. However, since the population continues to grow, albeit at a slower rate, the rural population has actually increased by 76 million.

The map shows the internal rate of urbanization in the countryside. This is part of a global trend: nearly half the world's population will reside in urban areas in 2000, and one person in six will live in cities with more than a million inhabitants (Pearson, 1998). China's urban population is not expected to exceed the rural population until 2025. The increasing urbanization is also a consequence of the reform policies, as people leave farming. In order to meet this, 600 new cities are to be built by 2011. Meanwhile, town and villages enterprises (TVEs) have absorbed an estimated 92 million people. More prosperous towns and villages are behaving like micro-states, keeping their populations in the countryside (Benewick, 1998).

In addition to the industrialization of the countryside, the reforms have created a huge mobile population of 120 million flocking to coastal provinces in search of employment (**Maps 5, 6, 19**). Since they are non-permanent residents, city populations are underestimated. Despite this redistribution of rural urban populations, the continuing intensity of population density on the eastern seaboard means that China's population remains unevenly spread across its territory (**Map 1**).

China's cities are most usefully understood as administrative centers with a very great concentration of populations. City administrative districts can be visualized as in concentric circles: the old city/inner city; suburban districts which contain district-administered towns; commune/market towns. Then, outside the urban area, but within the municipality, there are rural counties which contain county-administered towns and more market towns and communes. Cities include the province-level cities of Beijing, Shanghai, Tianjin and, most recently, Chongqing, which is touted as the largest city in the world; capitals of provinces or autonomous regions or state-planning cities such as Dalian (Liaoning) and Qingdao (Shandong Province), which are responsible to the central government. For the purposes of investment and development some, such as Dalian and Qingdao, are also designated as Open Cities, and a smaller number, such as Shenzhen, are Special Economic Zones.

Sources: Ian Pearson, ed, *The Atlas of the Future*, New York: Macmillan Inc; London: Routledge, 1998 • Robert Benewick, "Towards a Developmental Theory of Constitutionalism: The Chinese Care," *Government and Opposition*, Autumn 1998 • Richard Kirkby, *Dilemmas of Urbanization: review and prospects*, London: Longman, 1994 • press reports

3 The Gender Gap

Gender relations in China continue to be hampered by the priority given to men in social and cultural organizations. Although the importance of family life to a healthy nation is a common thread running through the 20th century – in the social policy of the Imperial, Republican and Communist regimes – there have been exceptional periods. In the late 1960s girls were encouraged by political idealism to put off marriage and sex, and in the 1970s the birth-control program placed an emphasis on the way people behaved in relation to the rest of the population, rather than in relation to their own sexuality or desire for a family. This policy was called the later-longer-fewer (*wan-xi-shao*) plan. Women would marry later, have longer spaces between births, and fewer children overall. In 1979 the one-child policy was announced: a system of rewards and fines, designed to significantly decrease the proportion of children to adults. In 1981 the policy was tightened to demand that all families should restrict themselves to a single child until the year 2000. The plan was that the size of the population would stabilize in the interval, without having a long-term effect on the composition of society. Unfortunately, the fundamental problem of gender inequality led to abusive practices against unwanted girl children.

Neither the Cultural Revolution of the 1960s, nor the delay of marriage in the 1970s had overturned the basic social assumption of male superiority, nor of women's imperative to be mothers and wives. There has been progress since Liberation (*jiefang*) in 1949, however. Women are now involved in public life, especially at local levels. The number of female deputies in the National People's Congress (**Maps 20, 21**) increased from 147 in 1954 to 626 in 1993. In 1993 there were 308 women mayors in the cities. The Communist Party of China has 7 million women members, 14 percent of the total membership. Many political women are, however, engaged in, or assigned to "women's issues", a situation which exacerbates gender divisions in the sphere of government. In the work force women still tend to occupy informal, part-time, and low-wage positions. Women who appear in statistics as "professional and technical", are generally nurses or teachers. These roles are respected, but carry less status and lower pay than many of the male-dominated professions.

Discrimination starts young. School enrolments (**Map 25**) are lower for girls than boys, especially in rural areas. Approximately 70 percent of illiterate people in China are women. The picture is different for urban single-child girls, where parental hopes and ambitions focus on their education, opportunity and material advantage. These girls are unlikely to be forced into unacceptable marriages, they will probably receive a tertiary education, and they are likely to achieve financial independence once they enter the work force. By a strange coincidence, some of the poorest and most disadvantaged women in urban areas also enjoy an enhanced economic independence. These are the migrant workers who send money back to their home villages, and thus to some degree transcend the stigma of womanhood in rural China.

The future of all these women is mixed. If the gender gap continues to widen there will be more violence against women as they become scarce, but undervalued "human commodities" in an increasingly market-oriented society. Some women will benefit from their single-child status, but this is not a significant factor, as intellectual and professional families have long taken the education of their daughters very seriously. Women will suffer if the employment rate drops, and men demand access to jobs in a shrinking field of opportunity. The gender gap is a symptom rather than a cause of women's struggles for equal status with men in public, economic and domestic life in China today. Women will need to increase their role in the building of governmental systems, in accessing economic power in the era of reform, and in avoiding the worst degradations of capitalism on their bodies and self-respect.

Sources: Tamara Jacka, *Women's Work in China: Change and Continuity in an Era of Reform*, Cambridge and Melbourne: Cambridge University Press, 1997 • Penny Kane, in "Population and Family Policies", Benewick and Wingrove (eds)., *China in the 1990s*, Basingstoke: Macmillan (revised 1998)

4 National Minorities

Although national minorities in China make up a small proportion of the population, because of the size of the overall population they comprise a very large number of people. Just one minority group, the Zhuang, are more numerous than the current population of Australia. The term, "national minority" (*zhongguo shaoshu minzu*), is based on a Stalinist definition of nationality: "an historically constituted community of people having a common territory, a common language, a common economic life, and a common psychological make-up which expresses itself in a common culture." (Wang, 1998) In theory, this definition works in favour of political citizenship, against a pan-Chinese ethnic identity. In practise, there are documented economic and social disadvantages attached to minority status for many groups.

Recognition of minority status currently applies to 56 groups, including the dominant Han majority. Despite the insistence on discrete national identities, there are many similar elements within the experience of many minority groups, whatever their "nationality". These can be summed up as: economic disadvantage, poor representation at national levels, religious repression and educational disadvantage. Direct repression is only encountered when the State perceives religion operating as a galvanizing force in demands for independence (as opposed to autonomy).

The most highly publicized case is that of Tibetan Buddhism. However, the situation in Xinjiang is, if anything, more troubling to central government. Xinjiang is known to Muslims in Central Asia as East Turkestan, a name which relates the predominantly Muslim Uighur population to their neighbours in newly independent states: Kirgistan, Kazakhstan, Uzbekistan, Tajikistan, and Turkmenistan. These were formerly part of the Soviet Union, but are recalled in the memory of their indigenous peoples as parts of a greater Turkestan that converted to Islam 1,200 years ago. Unrest is reported in Xinjiang and the problems may be as much to do with central government containment strategies as with the long-standing religious allegiance.

Large-scale migration of Han and other ethnic groups into Tibet and Xinjiang has produced a two-tier economic system, with the Tibetans and the Uighurs sitting at the bottom of the economic ladder in their own areas. Many of the incomers have been troops, stationed semi-permanently to reclaim wasteland and establish new oases. This policy, which echoes age-old centralist ideas of "strengthening frontiers through people" (*yimin shibian*), is dangerous to fragile environments but is also perilous for the people who find themselves washed osmotically out of the structure of development by better-educated and more highly skilled migrants. By 1996, 38 percent of inhabitants of the region were Han.

The dual-structure of the economy of Xinjiang, developed through Han and other ethnic immigration, is structured around modern industry in the north, and an agricultural base in the south. The Uighurs tend to reside in the poorer south, whereas recent migrant populations operate and expand in the north. There have been similar experiences in Tibet and Inner Mongolia, although not as obviously as in Xinjiang. Between 1964 and 1994, 70 percent of migrants into Tibet were themselves Tibetans from nearby provinces. Migrants into Inner Mongolia have been predominantly Han, but the proportion of Mongolians has remained stable. The situation is not simple, however. Key indicators still suggest economic disadvantage for minorities; life expectancy in Xinjiang is 65.7 years – as opposed to a national level of 69.81 years. This makes it the fourth lowest after Yunnan, Qinghai, and Tibet, all minority areas.

Sources: *The Cambridge Handbook of Contemporary China*, Chapter 9, p.205 • David Wang, "Han Migration and Social Changes in Xinjiang," *Issues and Studies*, vol. 34, no.7, July 1998, pp.33–61 • Zhang Tianlu Huang Rongqing, *Zhongguo shaoshu minzu renkou diaocha yanjiu (Surveys and Research into China's Minority Populations)*, March 1996, Gaodeng Jiaoyu Chubanshe; • Amir Teheri, "The Chinese Muslims of Xinjiang,"*Arab View*, <http://www.arab.net/> • "Promoting Three Basic Freedoms: Freedom of Association Assembly and Expression," September 1997 <http://www.igc.apc.org/hric/

5 Equality and Inequality

The people of China experience very different life-styles, according to the region in which they live, whether they are urban or rural, whether they are male or female, and depending on their access to the infrastructure necessary for economic development. Some of these differences are historical and geographical. The coastal provinces have easy access to trade by sea, a strongly developed urban network, and close connections with the seat of power in Beijing. Guangxi has been isolated by its topography and by its distance from the northern centre of power. It has suffered badly from floods, a population increase, high inflation and a decline in rural income levels. Large, predominantly rural, provinces, such as Qinghai, Gansu, Yunnan, and Guizhou are also disadvantaged by their distance from the center, by their low proportion of successful commercial activities, and by the slower rate of modernization which they experience. The government is working hard to develop these regions, and the increase in telephone subscribers in rural areas is an indicator of this resolve (**Map 30**). Guangxi is receiving special attention but many areas remain undeveloped and inaccessible. Many of the poorer regions in China are populated by national minorities (**Map 4**). This must give the Chinese government cause for concern. If the economic revolution continues, and the casualties of the market continue to increase, there will be a greater likelihood of disaffection amongst all rural communities, but particularly those in minority areas.

One solution is to devolve financial and fiscal powers to the provinces (*fangquan rangli*) in the hope of controlling resources, containing unrest, and developing economic links across China that are perceived to be equal and mutually profitable. The distribution of wealth across the provinces is complicated by the large income differentials within provinces. Rural counties, even those adjacent to one another, are experiencing varying levels of economic advantage. This may be another incentive to increasing provincial autonomy, which goes hand in hand with existing attempts to "match up" rich and poor provinces in an effort at poverty alleviation. This is known as "horizontal regional co-operation", (*hengxiang jingji lianxi*). All such plans, as well as fundamental attempts to reduce illiteracy and safeguard welfare provision (**Map 28**), are reliant on the continuing solvency of the nation's economy. If that is adversely affected by the slump in Asia, there may be more poverty, more division, and less stability across the entire region.

Sources: John Gittings, *Real China: From Cannibalism to Karaoke*, New York: Simon and Schuster, 1996 • Diana Hwei-an tsai "Regional Inequality and Financial Decentralization in Mainland China" I*ssues and Studies*, May 1996, pp. 40–71 • B. Andreosso-O'Callaghan and Wei Qian, "The PRC's Economy - From Fragmentation to Harmonization?", unpublished MS, 1997 • Christina P W Wong, "Central-local Relations in an Era of Fiscal decline: The Paradox of Fiscal Decentralization in Post-Mao China," *The China Quarterly*, Dec 1991, no. 128, pp. 691-715 • Ya-chun Chang, "The Financial Autonomy of Provincial Governments in Mainland China and Its Effects" *Issues and Studies*, vol. 32.3, March 1996, pp. 78-95 • Jae Ho Chung, "Beijing Confronting the Provinces," *China Information*, vol. IX, nos 2/3 (Winter 1994/5), pp. 1–23 •Feng-cheng Fu and Chi-keng Li, "Disparities in Mainland China's Regional Economic Development and Their Implications for Central-Local Economic Relations", *Issues and Studies*, vol. 32.11, November 1996, pp. 1–30 • Alan P.Liu, "Beijing and the Provinces: Different Constructions of National Development", *Issues and Studies*, vol. 32.8, August 1996, pp. 28–53

6 Employment

Employment is increasingly described in the same breath as its partner, unemployment. China is no exception in its response to the demands of capitalism and the global market. The nature and requirements of work in China are now very different from the years of peasant agriculture and heavy industry, supplemented by political and intellectual work. People have re-invented themselves as migrant laborers, service workers, small-scale entrepreneurs, and business managers. These changes are producing wealth for some, but uncertainty for many.

There are several factors contributing to new employment profiles in China: reform and modernization, recent history, and regional imbalance in capital distribution and labor costs. Unemployment surfaced in the late 1970s when tens of thousands of people in their twenties and early thirties returned to the cities from the countryside. These were "urblings", city youth who had spent much of their life since the age of 17 working in remote rural areas as part of the management of the Cultural Revolution. Their impact on the employment figures were, however, minimal in comparison with the influx of migrant peasants which they foreshadowed.

There is often a time gap between the causes and effects of changes to employment patterns, and the reform policy of the 1980s caused an excess of rural labor in the 1990s. Furthermore, a 1995 report suggested that the rural labor force at the time included a 60 percent surplus built into it. These surplus workers will "surface" in their turn as members of the floating population, or the dispossessed poor in their home provinces. Between 1978 and 1986 the rural workforce diminished by only 1.2 percent (3.11 million people). This was partly due to rural mechanization and economies of scale (introduced despite the disbanding of the collectives). Some unemployment was taken up by the formation of rural enterprises, and town and village enterprises.

There remain deep regional divisions. Coastal regions are capital intensive and highly mechanized. Labor is thus freed to supplement incomes with alternative and seasonal employment. Meanwhile, farm practises in remote regions are labor intensive but generate very low wages. Family members, often young women, need to move into towns and cities as guest workers to supplement the household income. They achieve a certain status through their shift into economic power, but their situation in the urban centres is often precarious. Development in industrial practices often, at least in the short term, leads to downscaling, re-organization, and the subsequent displacement and reconfiguration of the work force. The worst-hit areas are in the central and western regions, especially Wuhan and the enormous Chongqing, which sustains a population of over 30 million (**Map 2**).

Unemployment is not a totally new phenomenon in the People's Republic, but it is newly visible, due to the break-up of the welfare system and the pressures on the state-owned enterprises. These huge employers can no longer "mop up" surplus labor. Workers in state-owned industries are facing closures and the disappearance of welfare arrangements in their enforced retirement. Industry managers are seeking "bad loans" from banks in order to preserve employment as much as to restructure unprofitable enterprises; but this cannot continue. By May 1998 half of the designated SOEs had not yet undergone reform and restructuring, which they must do to survive at all.

New competition, and hopefully new employment opportunities, will come from the private sector. In March 1999 the National People's Congress endorsed private businesses as a legitimate part of the national socialist economy. Meanwhile, the number of workers that had been "stood down" (xiagang) continue to grow. A Chinese research team reported 13 million redundancies in 1997 and 20 million in 1998. A new category is emerging to swell these figures. These are contract workers who are still statistically "employed" but whose contract has expired and are paid only a portion of their wages if anything at all.

Women workers are particularly disadvantaged. Over half of newly laid-off workers are women, although they make up only one-third of the workforce. This adds to an already weak position for women, as only 46 percent were working for wages in the mid-1990s. Along with male urban dwellers, they are further challenged by the illegal, cheap labor on hand from poorer regions. Through this escalating hardship, political leaders and the trade unions are battling to preserve the population from the worst excesses of capitalist exploitation, but the possibility of exploitation, insecurity or employment and dangerous working conditions grows along with the market. The choice is being made between social problems and a strong national economy. It is still uncertain which way the state will move in the long term.

Sources: Yunhua Liu, "Labor Absorption in China's Township and Village Enterprises", Paper for the International Conference of Economics of Greater China, 1997 • "Zhongguo xinwen she," China News Agency, 2 May 1997 • "Women at Work", Asiaweek, February 28, 1997, 10 • Fang Shan, "Unemployment in Mainland China: Current Situation and Possible Trends," Issues and Studies, vol. 32, no.10, October 1996 • China Population Statistics Yearbook, China Statistical Publishing House,1998 • China Statistical Yearbook, China Statistical Publishing House,1998 • Lateline, ABC Australia, 16. March,1999 • John Gittings, "China puts its faith in enterprise", Guardian Weekly, March 21, 1999, page 7 •Jean-Louis Rocca, "Unemployment sweeps China", Le Monde Diplomatique (International edition), February 1999, pp. 6–8 • Lina Song, "The Determinants of Female Labor Migration in China: a case study of Handan", Institute of Economics and Statistics, Oxford University; paper presented SOAS; June 8, 1995 • Tamara Jacka, "Working Sisters Answer Back: The Presentation and Self-Presentation of Women in China's Floating Population", China Information, vol. XIII no. 1, Summer 1998, pp. 43–73

7 Agriculture

China is still a rural society. Despite rapid urbanization since the introduction of Deng Xiaoping's reform economy in early 1980s, most Chinese are part of a huge agricultural population. Agriculture is a shifting category however. China needs feeding, but the people involved in the production of basic foodstuffs are under threat. Much of the income earned by agricultural workers now comes from diversification, often small-scale enterprises conducted within the household. Rural enterprises vary in size and scope. The town and village enterprises are mainly collective, but there are also individual and partnership

concerns. Although these enterprises are consistently productive on a nationwide basis (**Map 8**), they do not employ a proportionate number of people. Rural workers who lack capital to join in with diversification are not advantaged by its success. As a result, many agricultural workers are giving up on the land altogether. They are moving to major towns and cities as part of the floating population of migrant workers (mangliu). They may find occasional work in the cities but at a price; wage differentials for urban employees and rural migrants in 1995 were 2.19:1. Many do not find work at all. Figures range widely, but a conservative estimation is that Beijing needs to create 18.6 million job opportunities every year to contain surplus rural and urban labor.

There are initiatives to modernize agricultural methods and maximize production in a terrain where only 7 percent of the land is suitable for agrarian use. Since 1978 engineers have been working on farm machinery that is adapted to the specific requirements of Chinese farmers. New hand-held tractors are now common where previously used Soviet machinery was uneconomic and unsuitable for small plots. Rice transplanters, combines, and grinders are all being produced and purchased in growing quantities. It is estimated that a household with diversification of income can recover the costs of machinery within two to three years of purchase. Attention is also focused on the production and use of pesticides. State investigations have demonstrated that 77.6 percent of pesticides are safe, according to current standards of acceptability. There remain large quantities of unsafe chemicals, mostly due to labelling problems, substandard formulas, and complicated distribution channels.

It is a priority to modernize safely, but the pressures are great in a period of uneven development. The land itself is under threat from short-term money-spinning development. The problem has been addressed by a 1997 promulgation to the effect that all agricultural land conversion was frozen for twelve months. The imperatives for the sustenance of China's agriculture was summed up in a national newspaper:

> This kind of disregard for the future of our country, for the life and death of our people, and for the well-being of our children and grandchildren cannot be tolerated! Everyone has responsibility for protecting farmland. We must take good care of the land that our ancestors have farmed for 5,000 years. Only in this way will we be able to answer the people in foreign countries who urgently ask, "Who will feed China in the 21st century?" China will answer confidently, "Our future is one of sustainable development. We will be able to rely completely on our own land to feed China and to build China." (People's Daily, May 19.1997)

Sources: Yunhua Liu, "Labor Absorption in China's township and Village Enterprises",unpublished paper at The International conference of Economics of Greater China (Perth 1997) • Fang Shan "Unemployment in Mainland China: Current Situation and Possible Trends", Issues and Studies, 32–10, October 1996 • "Agricultural Pesticide Use in China", "Irrigation in China Demands More Efficient Technologies", "Farm Mechanization in China", "The Environment enters the Chinese Criminal Code"
<http://www.redfish.com/USEmbassy-China/sandt/>

8 Industry

The industrial sector in China is rapidly diversifying. On the one hand there are still a large number of state-owned enterprises (SOEs), many with bad debts and production problems. It is estimated that in 1999 there will be a 50 percent rate of surplus manufacture, mainly from the SOEs. These industries employ and under-employ, and have in the past underwritten their workers' welfare from cradle to grave. Government services have been delivered through the auspices and institutions of industry. A relatively small number (512) of large enterprises, designated "pillar industries," will remain in state control for the forseeable future, however. This has as much to do with political considerations as with economic forces. Reforming these industries could involve shedding as much as one-third of their workforce, with potential consequences for political stability.

Meanwhile, private enterprises are being actively encouraged, and may soon have access to state bank loans. In some counties "attached" businesses, those which operate privately but are formally registered as public companies, are moving into an openly private classification. The mood is very much in favor of the professional entrepreneur, with some support given to state industries in acknowledgment of the work they do for welfare, if not for national solvency. Successful entrepreneurs tend to be young, flexible, willing to travel, and able to free themselves of the restraints of "connections" (*guanxi*). By contrast, corruption in small manufacturing industries is often linked to a hierarchy of entrenched political interests, and a whole web of immovable links and favors, rotting the system.

Many private factories are small, and products are concentrated geographically according to historical skills and trading links established under previous economic regimes. In one southern textile area in 1997 one village had 300 factories amongst 920 families. The benefits of these small and flexible units lie in their ability to respond to demands from a rapidly changing consumer market, and also to downsize fairly painlessly (except of course for the migrant workers who are used as extra labor in the good times). The danger of burgeoning private enterprise, but also of public enterprises under pressure to reform and perform, is very real. Safety in the workplace is not good. The incidents which brought the issue to international attention were the factory fires in Shenzhen and Zhuli in 1993. In that year alone 11,600 workers died in industrial accidents. Migrant workers (*min gong*) are most at risk in these situations. Many of them live in hostels run or leased by the factory, but with none of the state benefits administered by the SOEs. It is a mirror system that makes a mockery of the five guarantees for industrial labor.

Sources John Gittings, "China Puts its Faith in Enterprise," *The Guardian Weekly*, March 21, 1999 ●Linda Wong and Ka-Ho Mok, "Dynamism and Development: Economic Growth and Social Change in Post-Mao China," The Asian Journal of Business Administration, vol. 18, no..2, December 1996, pp. 201–33 ● Jonathan Unger/Anita Chan, "Inheritors of the Boom: Private Enterprise and the Role of Local Government in a Rural South China Township," Murdoch University Asia Research Centre Working Paper 89, 1999 ● Jonathan Unger, "The Rise of Private Enterprise in a Rural Chinese District," Murdoch University Asia Research Centre Working Paper 90, 1999 ● *Asian Wall Street Journal*, Leader, March 3, 1999

9 Services

The service sector was a political non-starter in the years before the reform era of the 1980s and 1990s. Maoist and statist perspectives downgraded service and emphasized production. Valid outlets for services have been through the public service provided by government agencies. The re-growth of service industries, particularly in southern China, has moved in fits and starts since the 1980s, and with varying degrees of transparency. Department stores selling luxury goods, upmarket restaurants, and late-night clubs are features of major cities. Hawkers are also common on city streets, but they need to be licensed. Those who come in from the countryside to sell off surplus produce have operated under "specialized agricultural households" licences. Those selling food or manufactured produce on city streets are also required to obtain "temporary business licences" (*linshi jingying xuhe zheng*). The penalty for non-compliance can be fairly straightforward. Police are quite likely to throw large piles of unlicensed produce into the canal.

The tourist industry is a major non-productive growth area in the Chinese service sector. Although pilgrimages and festival days have promoted internal travel across most periods of Chinese history, modern tourism is a recent development. Nevertheless, established private companies are already experienced enough to refine their developments in line with local and international expectations. Some companies are centred on villages lucky enough to be situated near a genuine "site". Villages in rural Beijing at the foot of the Great Wall have moved fast to develop service facilities (and hawking) to maximize the benefit of their proximity. Between 1949 and 1972 the wall was only accessible to "special friends of the Revolution" and only 250,000 visas were issued in those years. The wall is now a necessary part of any Beijing visitor's itinerary.

Other companies are promoting tourism by exploiting natural resources. Cave formations attract visitors to areas around Hangzhou and Guangzhou. As tourist sites are priced and licensed according to the number of attractions presented, cave management companies build wonderlands of lights, mythological theme parks, laser shows, and underground river trips into their programs. Developments in the early 1980s tended to be technologically simple. Successful companies are re-investing in high-tech light shows and amenities to remain competitive in a fierce market. In 1993 rival villages went into battle to protect their claims to local caves, such was the projected value of the tourist trade.

Despite the long-running international discomfort with China's presence in Tibet, there is a strong focus on the region to attract domestic (Han Chinese), and some international, tourists. Over 100,000 foreign visitors moved through the autonomous region from 1990–97, and exchange earnings grossed US$48 million. Lhasa is becoming the fulcrum of tourist routes across the plateau, and the region is investing heavily in roads and facilities to continue the trend.

Sources: Lynn T. White III, *Unstately Power: Vol .1. Local Causes of China's Economic Reforms*, New York: M. E. Sharpe, 1998 ● F. M. Sarah Li and H. B.

Trevor Sofield, "Tourism development and socio-cultural change in rural China", A. V. Seaton (ed.), *Tourism: The State of the Art*, Chichester: John Wiley & Son, 1994 • _____ "Historical Methodology and Sustainability: An 800 Year Old festival from China," *Journal of Sustainable Tourism*, forthcoming 1999/2000 • _____ "Is The Great Wall of China The Great Wall of China?" Paper given at the 14th World Congress of Sociology. Montreal, 1998 • Zhang Zhiping, "Exploration Tourism: A New Pursuit," *Beijing Review*, November 24–30, 1997, pp14–16.

10 Traffic

In 1952, 66.7 percent of travellers in China journeyed by rail. That had fallen to 8.8 percent by 1995 (although with only a fractional decrease in actual numbers travelling, owing to the massive increase in total population). Over the same period, highway traffic took up the dominant position, moving from 18.6 percent to 88.8 percent of domestic volume.

Motorized transport in China is still predominantly communal: buses and taxis are much more common than private cars. There is also a vast regional variation. In Beijing in 1996 there were 430,500 buses and cars on the roads. In Henan, a province with approximately seven times the population of Beijing, there were 236,900. The figures indicate even more discrepancies in rural areas, where there is an average of less than 1 vehicle per 100 households. Amongst rural households in the Beijing district the ratio rises to 4 vehicles per 100 households.

These kind of figures suggest that the rather hackneyed Western image of China – still trotted out in advertising campaigns – of bicycles clogging the city streets, is still fairly accurate. What the ads do not show is the diversity of traffic – from antiquated diesel trucks, to horsedrawn carts, to various colours, shapes and sizes of taxi-cabs – which shares frantic city traffic jams with the bicycles. It is arguably this diversity that causes many of the road traffic accidents in major cities and makes travelling by road in the countryside so hazardous.

As the map indicates, the main purchasers of cars are taxi companies, state-owned enterprises, joint enterprises, multinationals, hotel fleets, and government departments. The proportions may shift slightly in 1999, when government officials lose their access to cars.

China's investment in infrastructure since 1949, including roads, bridges, railways, power plants, and water conservation projects, has been considerable. The reforms era has seen an expansion in highways from 890,000 kilometres in 1978 to 2.2 million kilometres – well on target for 2.3 million kilometres in 2000. The length of railroad laid has only increased from 48,618 kilometres to 57,600 kilometres over the same period (including the Beijing–Kowloon railway line).

Investment and construction has been woefully inadequate for China's rapidly growing economy. The plan to invest over US$1 trillion in infrastructure over the next three years in order to stimulate the economy will be a partial corrective.

Sources: "The Road to Progress", *Asiaweek* May 9, 1997, p.10 • *China Statistical Yearbook*, 1997.

11 Energy

If present trends continue, the world will use more energy in 2010 than in the 1990s. Globally, the average increase will be just under 50 percent. China will share in this increased demand, but its percentage increase will depend on the rate of economic and population growth. The International Energy Agency estimates that the percentage of China's share in world energy demand will increase from 11 percent in 2000 to 13 percent in 2010. Coal will increase from 28 percent to 31 percent, oil from 6 percent to 8 percent and electricity and gas from 8.5 percent to 11 percent (Priddle, 1996).

China is a leading world energy producer and the world's largest producer of coal. Coal may be emperor, but it is not unproblematic. Eighty percent of coal is produced in the north and the west, far away from the rich, industrial, coastal provinces. Much of the coal is of secondary quality, produced in small, inefficient and dangerous mines. In addition to the environmental and health costs, coal contributes to the transportation bottleneck (**Map 10**) since is takes up more than 40 percent of rail freight and is shipped by river and sea as well.

The crucial question for China is whether its energy resources are sufficient to meet its growing needs. China is the fifth largest oil producer in the world, but it has moved away from self-sufficiency to become a net importer. Both off-shore production and oil-field explorations in Xinjiang province have proved disappointing. Natural gas, which makes up 2 percent of China's energy production, is also located in the remoter parts of China. Questions loom heavy over the Three Gorges Dam project as a solution for hydro-electric power (**Map 32**). Nuclear power now comprises 1 percent of total energy output, but is planned to increase to 2.5 percent in 2010 and 5 percent by 2020.

The dependence on coal, and the propsect of an energy deficit, have moved China beyond importing oil to shopping for oil fields abroad. They have acquired fields in Kazakhstan, Azerbaijan, Sudan and Venezuela (*Far Eastern Economic Review*, 26 February 1998).

Sources: Ian Pearson (ed) *The Atlas of the Future*, New York: Macmillan; London: Routledge, 1998 • Robert Priddle, "China's Long-term Energy Outlook," *China in the 21st Century*, OECD, 1996 • *Far Eastern Economic Review*, February 26, 1998.

12 Investment

Foreign direct investment (FDI) has been the motor of China's economic growth. China offered plentiful cheap labor, available land, minimal restrictions working conditions, an authoritarian government committed to market reforms, and potentially a huge domestic market. In turn, foreign firms created employment, supplied expertise and training, and brought technology. China gained economic growth and made new friends. Business executives can be counted as among China's best allies. They persuade governments to restrain their criticisms of China's human rights abuses and lobby for export liberalization.

There are now over 200 of the world's largest multinationals in China, including General Motors, Volkswagen, Coca-Cola and Hewlett-Packard. The peak period for FDI, however, was

1992 to 1995. The Ministry of Finance reported that 61 percent of the 56,000 foreign-invested enterprises lost money in 1997. The Asian economic and financial crisis has taken its toll; Chinese companies from Hong Kong, Taiwan, and Southeast Asia, which are among the biggest investors, have had to sort out their domestic arrangements before committing funds abroad.

China's response has been the overdue investment in infrastructure. Foreign investors have responded by seeking control of their joint enterprises or by setting up wholly controlled subsidiaries. An economic slowdown, however, is not to be equated with a standstill, and the inflow remains impressive. Much of the investment is long term. Moreover, investment from Taiwan is bucking the trend. This includes the pillar of Taiwan's prosperity – the electronics industry. As one prominent Taiwanese commentator surmised: "Mainland China doesn't want to damage our economy. But they are using economics to make unification happen." (*Far Eastern Economic Review*, March 25, 1999).

The concentration of FDI in the eastern coastal provinces, as highlighted by the map, has at least two important consequences. First, there has been an increase in the power of these provinces relative to the center, or, stated differently, there has been a de facto devolution of political power from central government to the provinces. Second, the disparities between the coastal and inland provinces have widened. What was meant as a temporary development is all too likely to become further entrenched.

Sources: *The Far Eastern Economic Review*, March 25, 1999 • press reports.

13 Trade

China's foreign trade has reached a crossroads. The map graphically displays the remarkable growth in trade since the open policy was declared in 1978. With the inclusion of the Hong Kong SAR, China ranked fourth among the world's trading nations in 1997. There has been a dramatic shift towards the export of manufactured goods. These include clothing and footwear, textiles, electrical appliances, telecommunications equipment, and textiles. There has also been a striking improvement in quality, and in the reliability of delivery, making Chinese goods more competitive on the world market.

Trade, however, does not take place in isolation. China has been seeking admission to the World Trade Organization (WTO) and its predecessor the General Agreement on Tariffs and Trade (GATT) for 13 years. Membership for China would involve greater transparency, acceptance of the "national treatment" principle, which restricts nations from treating foreign enterprises less favorably than domestic ones, and the reduction and withdrawal of trade barriers.

US support is crucial to China's admission to the WTO. There is mutual self-interest, for the USA has become China's single largest export designation, while China is the fastest-growing large export market for the USA (*Far Eastern Economic Review*, November 12, 1998). The Americans, however, are alarmed at the ever-increasing trade deficit with China, estimated at US$60 billion for 1998. China has

made concessions reducing duties on imports from 30 percent to 16 percent since 1990, and most recently has proposed further reductions in tariffs, greater foreign ownership in the telecommunications industry, easing restrictions on agricultural products and more freedom for foreign banks in China.

What lies behind the failure to gain admission to the WTO are a host of political conflicts, mainly between the USA and China. From the American point of view there are China's human rights abuses, the alleged theft of nuclear secrets, the buying of political influence and the military buildup against Taiwan. China fears American hegemony, their strategic alliances in Asia, and in 1999 opposed NATO's war in Yugoslavia. The relative downturn in its domestic economy, the far-reaching industrial and welfare reforms, a shaky banking system, and rising unemployment and social unrest cautions China's leaders against allowing further foreign competition in its domestic market. Meanwhile, American politicians exploit China for political and electoral advantage.

In a globalizing economy it seems untenable to exclude the fourth leading trading nation from the crucial international institution, the WTO.

Sources: Jude Howell, "Foreign Trade Reform and Relations with International Economic Institutions," C. Hudson (ed), *The China Handbook*, Chicago and London: Fitzroy Dearborn Publishers, 1997 • Michaela Eglen, "China's entry into the WTO with a little help from the EU," *International Affairs*, vol.73 no.3, 1997 • Stuart Harris, "China's role in the WTO and APEC" in David S. G. Goodman and Gerald Segal, *China Rising*, London and New York: Routledge 1997 • *Far Eastern Economic Review*, November 12, 1998 • press reports.

14 Greater China

Greater China is primarily, and most usefully, a demographic and economic concept. It tends to refer to Chinese populations both within China itself and those in Southeast Asia that have a developed commercial connection with the People's Republic. The idea of Greater China is that whatever political differences are at play, Chinese populations continue to consider one another as natural and viable partners in business and trade. There is also an underlying sense in which being Chinese in itself motivates some of these financial relationships.

It is scarcely surprising that Chinese investors from outside China (who contribute 80 percent of investment in China) are keen to support economic change and development in the motherland. As events in Indonesia in 1998 demonstrated, the economic success of some members of overseas Chinese populations is often punished rather than praised. It is a prudent and emotional decision to invest where one's money and ethnicity will be appreciated.

China itself is active in promulgating the notion of Greater China. Its usage is regional and strategic, frequently drawing together a triangle of southern China, Taiwan and Hong Kong–Macau. This informal grouping is developing in parallel with international organizations, such as Malaysian-led EAEC (East Asian Economic Caucus), ASEAN (which excludes Taiwan but is traditionally anti-Communist), and APEC (Asia-Pacific Cooperation Forum), which incorporates non-Asian countries into its scheme for inter-regional co-operation in the Pacific.

Greater China is sometimes a much larger concept, associated with the idea of diaspora. In this usage anyone of Chinese descent living anywhere in the world can claim ethnic, historical and cultural affiliation with all Chinese in and out of China.

Another concept associated with Greater China is the notion of the transnational. This takes into account the porous nature of relations between and across states and cultures. It is certainly a helpful way of evaluating the relationship between Taiwan and the Mainland, between Hong Kong and Taiwan, and between Singapore and Australia, to give only a few examples. Transnationalism can refer to economic dependency and co-operation, and also to cultural transfers and hybrids. It is an optimistic and productive version of cultural development, but has been viewed as ominous in the economic spheres. Transnational companies avoid the regulation of the nation-state, and the check of democratic process. On the other hand, they benefit from accrued capital, talent and a contemporary understanding of the global marketplace.

Sources J. H. Chang, P. Kee and J. Chang (eds) *Chinese Cultures in the Diaspora: Emerging Global Perspectives on the Centre and the Periphery* National Endowment for Culture and the Arts, Taipei, 1997 • R. Chow, *Writing Diaspora: Tactics of Intervention in Contemporary Cultural Studies*, Bloomington and Indianapolis: Indiana University Press, 1993 • Hoogvelt, Ankie, *Globalisation and the Postcolonial World: The New Political Economy of Development*, Basingstoke: Macmillan, 1997 • P. Kee, "The New Nanyang: Contemporary Chinese Populations in Australia" in J. H. Ong, K. B. Bun and S. B. Chew, (eds) *Cross Borders: Asian Transmigration*, Prentice Hall,1995, pp290–316 • P. Kee, "The Growth and Diversification of Australia's Chinese Community" in J.H. Chang, P. Kee and J. Chang (eds), *Chinese Cultures in the Diaspora: Emerging Global Perspectives on the Centre and Periphery*, National Endowment for Culture and the Arts: Taipei, 1997, pp. 139–153 • A. Ong and D. Nonini, *Ungrounded Empires: The Cultural Politics of Modern Chinese Transnationalism*, London: Routledge, 1997.

15 Chinese Communist Party
China is governed by a relatively small number of leaders who exercise power, both formally through a multiplicity of power structures and informally through a network of contacts. Viewed from this perspective, China does not differ from most nation-states. Yet it is radically different. As the most powerful of the few surviving communist states, the Party leadership refuses to entertain the possibility of a legitimated and institutionalized opposition. One of the legacies of the crackdown of the Tiananmen protest of 1989 is that the Party-state served notice that it would severely punish unauthorized mass movements and public demonstrations.

China's formal power structures include, first and foremost, the Communist Party. Other power structures include the government, the bureaucracy, the PLA, the judicial system including the police, and the provinces individually and collectively (including the Hong Kong Special Administrative Unit), but all of these power structures, although separate, are pre-eminently related to the Party. The structures of the Party parallel and penetrate those of the government, for example, and there is an overlap of personnel. The Party contends and proposes, the state amends and disposes.

The formal power structure, how power is exercised informally, and who exercises it can all be described in terms of a pyramid structure. This pyramid structure is also evident in the organization of the Party. There is a hierarchical relationship, concentrating power at the apex of the pyramid and exercising control down to the base. Democratic centralism may be the form providing the opportunities and avenues for debate and discussion at all levels of the Party to be communicated upwards, but decisions are transmitted downwards.

Rather than presenting the National Party Congress as the highest decision-making body in the Party (**Map 16**), as described in its constitution, a pyramidic representation of power shows that decision-making is concentrated in the Standing Committee of the Politbureau, who rule on behalf of the Party. An analysis of the membership of the Standing Committee demonstrates how power has passed from a generation of revolutionary and veteran leaders to a generation of technocratic leaders. Six of the seven members of the Standing Committee are trained as engineers and the seventh in business management. The analysis also reveals that three of the seven members simultaneously hold the highest ranking positions in the government and are at the apex of the power pyramids. Jiang Zemin is General Secretary of the Party, President of China and Chairman of the Central Military Commission; Zhu Rongji is Premier; and the former Premier, Li Peng, is Chairman of the Standing Committee of the National People's Congress.

Power and its exercise, however, is not always visible and in China much depends on the base of support, personal and institutional. Hence, Li Peng is usually ranked above Zhu Rongji as the second most powerful person in China, behind Jiang Zemin. Deng Xiaoping, however, was the most powerful leader in China even when he held no official position. In popular esteem, he was the paramount leader.

Sources: The authors • Colin Mackerras, et al (eds), *Dictionary of the Politics of the People's Republic of China*, London and New York: Routledge, 1998 • Shiping Zheng, *Party vs State in Post-1949 China*, Cambridge: Cambridge University Press, 1997 • Tony Saich, "China's Political Structure" in Robert Benewick and Paul Wingrave (eds), *China in the 1990s*, revised edition, Basingstoke: Macmillan 1999 • Yoshifumi Makai (ed) *China's Roadmap as seen in the 15th Party Congress*, Tokyo Institute of Developing Economies, 1998

16 Central Government
Twenty-one years of reform have been mainly devoted to the creation of a market-oriented economy. Although this has meant that there is a serious disjuncture between economic and political reforms, the latter, though often unacknowledged, are significant. These include some devolutions of power to the provinces, restrictions on tenure in high political office (causing Li Peng to step aside as Premier after serving two five-year terms); the streamlining of the bureaucracy through the introduction of measures to improve the quality of its personnel and, most recently, to reduce the number of ministries from 41 to 29; and the separation of the party from enterprise management. The political reforms contribute to a process of stripping away the foundations of a Leninist state, necessary to the development of a constitutional system and the institutionalization of power.

China's constitutional development is likely to be difficult and uneven. Although the end-product of this development cannot be predetermined, the chances are that it will be better suited and more adaptable to China's needs than a constitution grafted on as a result of a "big bang" approach to constitution-making which assumes that, once drafted and promulgated, the transition to democracy will follow. The 1982 constitution, the fourth since the founding of the People's Republic in 1949, has been amended several times to reflect the market-oriented economy and, most recently (**Map 21**), to strengthen the position of private enterprise and to incorporate the rule of law.

A pyramidic representation of China's central government provides a clearer picture of the power structures than the constitution affords. Firstly, China's government can be seen to possess those functions commonly associated with a political system: executive, legislative and judicial. Secondly, it is possible to identify those characteristics that are special to China, in particular, the Standing Committee of the National People's Congress (NPC) and the State and Party's Central Military Commissions. Thirdly, while the constitution specifies the National People's Congress as the highest organ of state power it is replaced here by the State Council in respect to the exercise of power. Fourthly, rather than a separation of powers or functions, the branches of government are shown to be linked and in an order according to the power they exercise.

The constitutional designation of the NPC as the highest organ of state power has led commentators to focus on what it does not do rather than what it does do. Too often, it has been dismissed as a rubber stamp legislature that meets once a year to hear the reports of state (and party) leaders. Certainly, the indirect election of its 2,979 members undermines its authority and independence.

Since the mid-1980s, however, the NPC has been attempting to assert its authority. First, its cause has been championed by three successive chairmen of the Standing Committee, appointed from the upper echelons of the party-state power structure during this period. The present chairman, the former premier, Li Peng, is in a position to further or to curtail this process. Secondly, the economic reforms have been generating a growing volume of legislation which is being met by a rise in professionalism and institutional resources. Thirdly, there have been changes in legislative behaviour in so far as a sizable number of delegates are beginning to propose amendments to legislation, delay legislation, withhold unanimous approval of appointments and work reports, and introduce their own items for consideration. Fourthly, there is evidence of lobbying mainly by the delegates on behalf of the local interest. Fifthly, the Standing Committee, which meets on a regular basis between the annual sessions of the NPC, is a working body. When the performance of China's incipient legislature is compared with that of more mature legislatures, the development of the NPC stands up reasonably well. When compared with the State Council it is clearly subordinate, but this is not out of line with executive-legislative relations elsewhere.

17 The People's Liberation Army

The post-Maoist reforms have not left the People's Liberation Army (PLA) untouched. In part they have involved a drive towards modernization and professionalization of the military. They have also brought it into contact with the temptations offered by the market-oriented economy.

The Chinese White Paper on National Defense of 1998 states: "During the new historical period the Chinese Army is working hard to improve its quality and endeavouring to streamline the army the Chinese way, aiming to form a revolutionized, modernized and regularized people's army with Chinese characteristics." Most dramatically, this means a reduction in the size of personnel from 4.3 million at the beginning of the reform era in 1978 to a planned 2.5 million in 2000. It is likely, however, that the million-strong People's Armed Police, charged with maintaining internal security and public order, and upgraded since the crackdown of the Tiananmen protest of 1989, has absorbed some of the loss of PLA personnel. Yet mounting unemployment may force the planners to think again about the proposed cuts.

Increases in defense expenditure are also involved, pointing to the improvement in military hardware and technology, including the purchase of weapons systems from abroad. Although the White Paper states that defense expenditure has declined as a proportion of total state expenditure, the real figures for defense spending, as is the case for most nations, are difficult to measure.

The map also refers to the PLA's involvement in the economy, and in particular production for civilian consumption. This dates back to PLA traditions of self-sufficiency and of contributing to its own upkeep, which has gained encouragement and momentum from the market reforms. It has been well placed to engage in the production of market goods through its command of resources and through the contacts with buyer and seller that it has built up. The market-oriented economy and the opening up to foreign trade has presented the PLA with unrivaled opportunities. In 1997 military exports were valued at US$7 million, half of which was from civilian products.

The question is raised whether or not the PLA's modernization drive and economic activities complement or conflict with each other. A 1994 report argued that the PLA, in having to engage in commercial activities to supplement the defense budget, was in danger of placing business interests above national security (*Far Eastern Economic Review*, August 6, 1998). Moreover, these profit-seeking pursuits divert resources from defense production. The government did not respond to this concealed warning until 1998. President Jiang Zemin went public, ordering the PLA to withdraw from civilian production and entrepreneurial activities. In addition, a clampdown on the PLA's smuggling activities was authorized as part of a wider campaign. It was estimated that the PLA's involvement in smuggling cost the government US$12 billion in lost revenue, that it was having a destabilizing effect on the economy, and that it was damaging the viability of the state-owned industries (*China News Digest*, July 25, 1998).

First steps have been taken to extract the PLA from its large number of business interests and to assert state control over its civilian production. Less clear is how it will be compensated for the potential loss of revenue, which accounts for about one-third of the defense budget. It is clear, however, that the PLA stands indicted for benefiting from the modernization drive, while its commercial pursuits undermine it. This has led one expert to remark, "In order to modernize, China's military is going to have to undergo an almost complete reconception of its role." (David Shambaugh, quoted in the *International Herald Tribune*, August 20, 1998)

Sources: *White Paper on China's National Defense*, Information Office, State Council of the People's Republic of China, 1998. BBC Summary of World Broadcasting, FE/3291/S3// July 29, 1998 ● China News Digest <CND.INFO@CND.ORG> ● *Far Eastern Economic Review* ● Godfrey Kwok-yung Yeung, "The People's Liberation Army and the Market Economy", Robert Benewick and Paul Wingrove (eds), *China in the 1990s*, London: Macmillan; Vancouver: University of British Columbia Press, revised edition 1999 ● "China's Military in Transition", T*he China Quarterly*, June 1996

18 Military Power

Western fear of Chinese military might is partly a product of the Cold War, partly a factor of racism, and partly an acknowledgment of the size of the population. This is despite the disparity in military spending between the USA and China. In 1997 US military expenditure accounted for 35.8 percent of the world total, and China's for only 4.5 percent. There should be little doubt, however, that China is an emerging military power, and as such is committed to the use of military force in the last resort. Military power and political positions in the Party are closely aligned in the administration of the Chinese State. The President of the People's Republic, Jiang Zemin is the Chairman of the Central Military Committee, a position similar to that of the US President as Commander in Chief of the armed forces. The two Vice-Chairmen, Chi Haotian and Zhang Wannian, are also in the Politburo. Their position is to match strength with negotiation in international affairs. One recent decision was the introduction of new rules of engagement in recognition of the nature of modern, high-tech, regional warfare. In the same month the Committee also approved the signing of a treaty (December 31, 1998) with the International Atomic Energy Agency (IAEA), agreeing to provide the Agency with information regarding China's arms trade with non-nuclear countries, as well as an undertaking to provide responses to queries raised by such countries about China's capabilities.

These agreements are made in the context of the Chinese "Five Principles of Peaceful Co-existence". Under that umbrella the Foreign Ministry cites the expansion of Chinese good relations with its near neighbour Russia, exchange visits made between President Clinton of the USA and President Jiang of China, the first presidential visit to China (in November 1988), and an increase in diplomatic harmony: China now officially recognizes, and is recognized by ,163 countries – which compares well with the 110 before 1978.

China's relationship with Taiwan, its nearest rival, is never comfortable, as the Republic's Government insists on Taiwanese autonomy, while the People's Republic demands

Taiwan's formal return to Chinese sovereignty. The map shows Taiwanese inferiority in military power, but the paranoia which fuels the state of readiness of such a small island reinforces the international perception that it may be only a matter of time before the two armies engage in conflict. That said, Taiwan has decreased defense spending over the past 30 years. The Taiwan effect received a new twist in 1999 when a Taiwanese-American (Wen Ho Lee) was suspected of giving information on highly mobile nuclear warheads to the Mainland.

Events such as this re-focus attention on the central world military relationship: between the USA and the People's Republic. China has other tensions closer to home, however. There have been border clashes with India (1987–88), and there are continuing arguments over rights to the Spratly islands (also claimed by Brunei, Vietnam, Malaysia, Philippines and Taiwan). China's recent, much-disputed nuclear tests infuriated Japan, once a sworn enemy and now a source of aid and trade. Including its first test in 1964, China had conducted 44 controlled explosions up to the end of July 1996, when they announced a suspension of testing. The test on August 17, 1995 created a small earthquake measuring 5.6 on the Richter scale. It took place two weeks after the 50th anniversary of the Hiroshima explosion. Along with the French Mururoa explosions in September that year, the timing was a painful reminder to the world that global military powers do not respect history in their pursuit of strength and "supreme national security".

Sources: *China Aktuell/China Monthly Data*, December 1998; January 1999 ● Foreign Minister Tang Jiaxun, quoted in *Beijing Review*, December 28, 1998–January 3, 1999, pp. 8–10 ● *Republic of China Yearbook* ● "Espionage: the Big Nuclear Giveaway," *Time*, March 22, 1999, pp. 28–29 ● "Nuclear Weapon Decision-Makers on the World Wide Web," Oxford Research Group information release, April 1998 ● Malcolm Lamb, *Directory of Officials and Organisations in China*, Contemporary China Papers: ANU, London: M.E. Sharpe, 1994 ● Dan Smith, *The State of War and Peace Atlas*, Penguin, 1996 ● Lisbeth Gronlund, David Wright, Yong Lui, "China and a Fissile Material Production cut-Off," *Survival*, The International Institute for Strategic Studies, Winter 1995–96 ● "Trust and Verify", *The Bulletin of the Verification Technology Information Centre*, no. 51, October 1994 ● *The Independent*, August 18, 1995

19 Beijing and Shanghai

Beijing and Shanghai stand out from China's 668 cities, from the 200 Chinese cities with populations of over 2 million, and from Tiangin and Chongqing as provincial-level cities, as centers of power. They are also the two cities of China that are best known internationally.

Beijing is an ancient Chinese capital, having served almost continuously as the residence of China's rulers since the end of the 13th century. The grandeur of the Imperial Palaces, the Temple of Heaven and the Great Wall, and the millions of tourists they attract testify to its power. The anti-Japanese and civil wars of the 20th century displaced Beijing as the capital until the People's Republic was declared in 1949.

Tiananmen Square is the symbol of New China and its new power, although the rulers live and work in Zhongnanhai, a compound not far away. Before 1949, Tiananmen was not a square but an imposing and intimidating forecourt to the Imperial Palace. Following the overthrow of the Qing dynasty in 1911 the forecourt was opened to traffic and became a focal point for political protests, most notably, the May 4 (1919) demonstration against the humiliation of the Versailles Treaty. Today, Tiananmen Gate, where the establishment of the People's Republic was announced and from where a portrait of Mao Zedong towers, forms the north end of the square. The monumental History Museum and the Great Hall of the People, where the National People's Congress meet, face each other across the square. On a north–south axis from Tiananmen Gate are the Monument to the People's Heroes and the Chairman Mao Memorial Hall, a Lincoln Memorial look-alike. Collectively, they articulate a statement of power.

The square is probably best known, however, for its open space. It is where people massed in 1949 to hear Mao Zedong declare the People's Republic; it is the venue for national celebrations and where Mao reviewed the Red Guards during the Cultural Revolution. Tiananmen Square was also the site of the student protests in 1989, against abuses of power, and near where the students experienced the wrath of the PLA crackdown.

Beijing benefits culturally and educationally from being the capital. In addition to being China's number one tourist destination, it hosts the China Peking Opera Company, the prestigious State Conservatory of Music, the Central Academy of Fine Art, China's Academy of Science, the Chinese Academy of Social Sciences and a large number of universities, including Beijing University, Qinghua University and the Chinese People's University. Beijing is more than a capital city, however, for it has a large industrial sector with heavy, as well as light, industry, producing iron and steel, machine tools, chemicals and electronics.

While Beijing is China's political capital, Shanghai ranks as China's economic capital. It is the largest single provincial-level contributor to central funds. Its own development lagged behind the national rate until Deng Xiaoping's famous Southern Tour of 1992, in the wake of the Tiananmen crackdown, sparked a revival in economic growth. Shanghai, in particular, benefited through preferential policies. Since then, it has been "face-lift city". Most spectacular has been the development of the Pudong Special Economic Zone across the river from the historic Bund, the pre-World War II centre of Asian capitalism. The intention is to establish Shanghai as a world leader in trade, finance and industry.

Pudong's potential glitz may be misleading, however, for most of Shanghai has undergone, and is still undergoing, transformation. This includes huge investments in infrastructure, the creation of cultural centres that rival Beijing, and the replacement of traditional industries and plant with modern industries and services. Shanghai has served as a stepping-off point to national leaderships; both President Jiang Zemin and Premier Zhu Rongji, for example, were former mayors. But Shanghai's power has been economic and it is likely to continue to be so.

Sources: Colin Mackerras, et al (eds) *Dictionary of the Politics of the People's Republic of China*, London and New York: Routledge, 1998 • Ellen Johnston Laing, *The Winking Owl*, Berkeley: University of California Press, 1988

20 The Center and the Provinces

The post-Maoist reforms have produced considerable tensions between the center and the provinces. It is clear, however, that increased local autonomy should not be mistaken for separatism, provincial realignments, or the possibility of federalism (even with Chinese characteristics) in the near future. China is very much a unitary party-state.

Even so, a shift in power from the center and towards the provinces, and between provinces, followed fiscal decentralization and the rapid economic growth of the coastal provinces in particular, with their ability to attract direct foreign investment (**Map 12**). The center has attempted to reassert its authority through the introduction of a new tax-sharing system in 1994, which has met with mixed success, by reducing provincial inequalities through policies which enjoin the prosperous provinces with the development of the interior (**Map 5**).

A second feature of local autonomy has been the growth of extra-budgetary revenue to a size where it almost equals budgetary revenue. The imposition of local taxes and fees, however, is increasingly encountering local resistance.

A third feature of local autonomy is the development of village governance or micro-states. A number of reforms have resulted in de facto political decentralization from the center. The map shows that party and state structures extend in parallel from the center to the grassroots and that both party and state reproduce themselves at each level. The general principle is that the government at each level is responsible both to the one above and to the party at its own level. There have been a number of changes since 1978, however. First, at the provincial and county levels, standing committees of people's congresses were instituted to supervise, in particular, the work of the government. Secondly, local people's congresses also elect their local government leaders and enact local laws and regulations. Thirdly, direct elections have been extended upwards to the county-level people's congresses. As is the case for the National People's Congress, people's congresses are no longer simply rubber-stamp legislatures.

The most dramatic change is the acquisition and exercise of considerable power by the more prosperous villages. Increasingly, they have assumed responsibility for the regulation and protection of property rights and as such behave as micro-states. Some commentators credit this to the decline of the Communist Party at the grassroots level, but it is more likely due to the combination of the improvement of the conditions of life for China's 900 million peasants, the development of town and village enterprises (TVEs) (**Maps 2, 11**) and the empowerment of elected village committees.

There have been three rounds of nationwide elections, involving over one million villages, since 1988. The elections have been growing more competitive and the use of the secret ballot is not uncommon. Where villagers have suffered, or at least have perceived there to be, abuses of power and mismanagement of resources, they have not hesitated in voting established and party leaders out of office. In addition to elected village committees, representative village assemblies are being created and village constitutions are being drafted.

It is important to note that village committees exist below the township, or basic, level of government. Yet village committees are involved in the development of local economies and in the provision of services and welfare. Where the villages are prosperous, usually as the result of successful TVEs, the village committees have considerable resources at their disposal, which can lead to intense political debate about their distribution.

Sources: Robert Benewick, "Towards a Developmental Theory of Constitutionalism: the Chinese Case," *Government and Opposition*, Autumn 1998 • David S G Goodman (ed), *China's Provinces in Reform*, London and New York: Routledge, 1997 • Barbara Krug, "Why Provinces? Diversity, Institutional Change and Decentralization," *Provincial China*, October 1997 • Colin Mackerras, et al (eds), *Dictionary of the Politics of the People's Republic of China*, London and New York: Routledge, 1998.

21 Rule By Law

The National People's Congress (NPC) at its annual meeting in March 1999 amended the constitution to incorporate the rule of law. The same session deleted the clause on "counter-revolutionary crimes", although some observers argue that political dissent is re-coded as "activities endangering state security".

An amendment is not enough to enshrine the rule of law in the constitution, however. This may be some way off insofar as the behaviour of judicial officials is indicative of institutional corruption. Corruption of judges and prosecutors in China, as elsewhere, is widespread. The president of the Supreme People's Court in his statement to the NPC admitted that "serious problems exist" including "illegal enforcement of laws, breaking regulations, torture or illegal interrogation of suspects, the arrest of witnesses" (*International Herald Tribune*, November 3, 1998). The figures presented by the President of the Court and by the Chief Prosecutor, following a year-long campaign against corruption and incompetence, are staggering. They reported that 2,512 judges and staff had been convicted of abuses of power, a rise from 1,051 in 1997; 1,401 prosecutors and staff were disciplined or prosecuted; and more than 4,200 para-judicial workers were sacked. More than two-thirds of over 40,000 officials investigated for corruption, involving a total of at least US$534 million, were indicted.

The procuratorate has been targeted by the NPC over a number of years and in 1997 only 55 percent of the deputies approved its annual report. The new Chief Prosecutor, Han Zhubin, has gained support through his dismissal of the Director and Deputy Director of the Anti-Corruption Bureau.

Corruption was a major cause leading to the Tiananmen protests of 1989 and it heads the lists of grievances of ordinary Chinese. Popular discontent has been further fuelled by accidents caused by poorly constructed roads and bridges. Neglect and oversight threaten the government's ambitious infra-structure programme to stimulate the economy and to create jobs, but also must raise doubts about implementing the rule of law in the near future.

The reports to the NPC, however, demonstrate that the Chinese leadership is taking corruption seriously. The development of a body of law and of a legal system is accepted as crucial to China's economic modernization. This is accompanied by the rapid growth and professionalization of the legal system. The number of law offices has grown from 3,716 in 1989 to 8,441 in 1997, and similarly the number of lawyers has increased from 34,379 to 98,902 over the same period.

Sources: press reports

22 State versus Citizens

The title "State versus Citizens", rather than the more widely recognized "Citizens versus State", signifies how difficult it is for China's leadership to translate its own view of human rights as well as its commitment to international standards into legislative provisions and judicial behaviour. Attention is also drawn to the need for the existence of organizations between citizens and the state, but independent of the state.

The explanation lies not only in China's traditional bias in favor of the state but also in the paradox of the market. The socialist market economy is not, as some would believe, a contradiction in terms. Yet the market does shift the emphasis away from collective and towards individual rights and values, and away from self-sufficiency and towards international inter-dependence and co-operation. The market creates interests, domestically and internationally, and these interests demand and, indeed, need to be heard and expect the state to respond. Market behaviour extends beyond the economy into the formation of citizens' organizations. In China these may be under the leadership of the Communist Party, state registered organizations or unofficial bodies.

The market, however, also creates new complexities which may threaten state authority and entrenched interests. This new environment of economic openness could engender political volatility. Rather than risk destabilizing conflicts, the Chinese leadership has chosen to promote political stability and the maintenance of public order. In the absence of institutional channels and recognized procedures, such as an independent judiciary and due process of law, the Party-state has resorted to authoritarian means, undermining both human rights and the market values it seeks. The persecution of the relatively small number of political dissidents and intellectuals is one example. The range of crimes punishable by the death penalty and the number of executions that take place is another.

China's trading partners can overlook or dismiss abuses of international standards of human rights in favor of market access and stability. Yet the paradox of the market holds. If China wants international acceptance it will not be able to continue to defy international standards. Although China by no means stands alone as the only state responsible for human rights abuses, as Amnesty reports make clear, it is cast as a pariah among states, particularly when it suits the interests of nations or interests within those nations. This is the case even though it is apparent that reports of the conditions of the labor reform camps (*laogai*), however grim, have been exaggerated, and that political prisoners only make up a small proportion of those incarcerated.

Sources: James D Seymour and Richard Anderson, *New Ghosts, Old Ghosts: Prisons and Labor Reform Camps in China,* Armonk, New York, M E Sharpe, 1998 • Gordon White, et al, *In Search of Civil Society,* London, Macmillan, 1997

23 Feeding China

The publication of Lester Brown's *Who Will Feed China?* in 1995 fuelled panic at the prospect of a large Chinese population unable to subsist within China's borders. Brown's analysis implied mass migrations and humanitarian catastrophes across Asia by the middle of the 21st century. More measured projections suggest that, whilst China is likely to increase grain imports from the USA and Australia in the first years of the new century, the rate of shortfall will not be as catastrophic as Brown predicted. This is predicated on government regulation and support for grain production against short-term cash crops and rice. This will have an effect on the export market in soya bean, peanuts, and vegetables, and possibly also on domestic consumption of these foodstuffs.

There is already a trend towards the consumption of meat protein over vegetable proteins and vegetables, due to higher household incomes and developments in trade and advertising. One very visible result of the socialist market, is the growth of fast-food outlets, where marketing is prioritized over dietary requirements. The meat market will have a subsidiary effect on grain imports, as animal feed will also need to be supplied. There has been a significant increase in the consumption of fish and other aquatic foods, however, many of which are produced as sidelines to traditional agriculture.

Grain still remains the key to self-sufficiency and stability in new China, however. Issues of storage, subsidy and distribution are high on the agenda of government. The grain market system encompasses two national, twelve regional, hundreds of local and 10,000 grain retail networks (Liao, 1994). The system is integrated with a storage policy which needs to be developed in line with production, and consumption as the population increases. The need for a long-term focus on grain management can be understood in a comparison with the eating habits of "developed" Taiwan; between 1992 and 1994 Taiwanese households consumed half the amount of grain as did households in the PRC, but twice as much meat, four times as much milk, and six times as much fruit. The trends in China may be away from a familiar food economy, but the emphasis for such a large, predominantly rural, population must still be the availability and price of grain.

The Chinese government is taking steps to meet the situation. An agricultural action plan was announced in March 1999, based on *China Agenda 21,* which was originally published in 1994, following the 1992 United Nations Conference on Environment and Development. The aim is to achieve sustainable growth in grain production, animal husbandry, fisheries and township enterprises. The first 36 projects include a food security warning system,

water and soil conservation initiatives and animal and plant conservation. In order to feed a predicted 1.6 billion people in 2030 an annual grain supply of 640 million tons will be needed. The crucial issue may be one of reliable statistics. As indicated on the map, the available arable land may have been seriously underestimated and if this is the case, together with increases in productivity, China should be able to meet its food needs. Against this is the tendency of local officials to exaggerate grain production.

Sources: Lester R. Brown, *Who Will Feed China?,* New York: W.W. Norton and Co., 1995 • Wen S. Chern, "Projecting Food Demand and Agricultural Trade in China," *The Asia–Pacific Journal of Economics and Business,* vol.1, no. 1, 1997 • Liao Shaolian, "Food production in China," *China Currents,* vol. 5, no. 4, Oct–Dec 1994, pp. 24–27

24 Households

The composition of households is demarcated along the rural–urban divide. Rural households are more likely to have extended-family living arrangements, whilst urban households are tending towards single-income households with only two generations living under the same roof. As a result, the problems and advantages of family life are different. Rural families still tend to arrange marriages according to family advantage rather than personal preference. The relationship between mothers-in-law and daughters-in-law is therefore a cogent issue in village life. Competition over household territory and emotional loyalty from son/husband fuels resentment and cruelty between women living in close proximity. In the mid-1980s the Women's Federation (*Fulian*) organized training sessions for young women to learn how to tolerate and accommodate the older woman in their lives. Meanwhile, domestic violence is an acknowledged but unsolved factor in household relations. In urban areas divorce is on the increase, as is the incidence of single-motherhood in the wake of failed marriages. These social phenomena, so familiar to Westerners, are accompanied by an equally familiar onus placed on women after the fragmentation of family units.

There have been public discussions of roles in the household. These concentrate on women's necessary "tolerance" of male needs, with men "helping out" with the chores "occasionally". The tensions in the household that inspire these discussions are exacerbated by the scarcity of living space for urban families. In 1997 a rural family had 2.5 times more living space per occupant than urban households. Urban families often live in housing blocs owned by the state enterprise where they are employed. Thus, a film director will live in a flat in the Beijing Film Studios' housing complex, whilst a textile worker will live with other textile workers in housing adjacent to the factory. There are exceptions to this form of housing allocation, but the problems associated with private landlords are replicated where state enterprises are losing money rapidly; capital is needed to keep the business afloat rather than maintain accommodation standards for the workforce. That said, urban families are more likely than rural households to have modern sewerage, adequate drainage, and access to piped water.

The single most significant change in the composition of

households across the whole of China has been the one-child policy of 1981. Single children are a normal sight in city streets, and to a lesser extent in rural areas, where the policy was amended to a maximum of two children in 1984. Minority peoples were given even higher maximums (three to four children). This may change as methods of implementation are amended. Where enforcement (sterilization and abortion) was common in rural districts at the height of the policy, now persuasion and education is advocated strongly. In urban areas the policy has also been relaxed, allowing those families willing to pay a high levy for the privilege of having a second child.

Sources: Emily Honig and Gail Hershatter, *Personal Voices: Chinese Women in the 1980's*, Stanford University Press, 1988 • Florence Beaugé, "Women's birth right", *Le Monde Diplomatique*, February 1999, p.9

25 Education

In the first decades of the socialist era education was strongly aligned with ideological training, political development, and the formation of good citizens for New China. This approach to the upbringing of China's youth was in conformity with general concerns in Chinese society and culture. Education (*jiaoyu*) is an essential component of childhood in Chinese life. Children's films, books, outings, must all have a demonstrable educational aspect. In practical terms, giving a working education to China's children is a difficult task. Private education is one of the solutions chosen by parents with the money to pay for it. The Fourteenth Congress of the Chinese Communist Party (1992), made this easier by its endorsement of "the socialist market economy".

As inequalities deepen in the wake of market reforms, some parents pay out huge sums for private schools and semi-private institutions (*minban*). In 1956 private schools were abolished as part of the reforms of Liberation. By the end of 1993 there were 125 different kinds of private school in Guangdong. Meanwhile, 80 percent of a total of 1 million primary schools have established enterprises through which to better their financial situation. Other children cannot attend school at all when family farming commitments require their labor, or when finances cannot stretch to the cost of fees and books. A developing tend towards streaming exacerbates the disadvantage of children with interrupted or incomplete schooling. Junior High school students (*chuzhong*) are streamed so that some are moved straight into vocational training whilst others continue into senior high, and consequently enjoy a more extensive set of options. This is a consequence of class and family opportunity, but also of gender. Figures demonstrate that whilst extremely clever girls do push forward into senior high, middle range female students do not. Despite scoring as well as, or better than, boys at high school entrance exams, far fewer girls actually enrol. The ratio at this level of attainment is 4 boys to each girl

As a developing nation China can claim reasonable rates of literacy (80 percent), although they are low when compared to Greater Chinese populations in Hong Kong (91.5 percent) and Taiwan (92 percent).

The tertiary sector is also growing fast. In 1984 the English language China-Europe Business School (CEIBS), China's first international business school, opened with the support and sponsorship of international firms as well as the local Shanghai Jiatong University. CEIBS is unusual in having an accredited MBA programme. 4,000 people applied for 120 places in the 1997 admissions round. In contrast to students during the Mao era, contemporary students are looking for choice and vocational, technical and commercial relevance in their education. Courses are no longer proscribed, they are marketed. Students at a Chemical Institute in Hading look at the courses and quality of teaching that is on offer, and choose which, and who, they prefer.

There is also a trend towards specialized education at higher and tertiary levels. Sichuan University offers courses in real estate, marketing, advertising, and interior decoration. Fudan in Shanghai concentrates on general business skills: accountancy, enterprise management, municipal planning and economics. These courses are self-financing and very popular. There are noticeable gender imbalances in the type of courses taken. Women make up a third of those in tertiary education. Many of them are concentrated in teacher training colleges. Chinese students are seeing the necessity of skills for a modern workplace, and those that can afford it are taking up the challenge.

Sources: *Guangdong Education Committee Yearbook*, 1994 • Mok Ka-ho, "Privatization and Quasi-Marketization: Educational Development in Post-Mao China", Department of Public and Social Administration, City University of Hong Kong, Public and Social Administration Working Paper 1996/4 • Zhang Wei, "The Movie Programme", CCTV, personal correspondence, 1998 • "China Survey", *The Economist*, March 8, 1997, 17–19 • Cesar Becani, "Becoming a Foreigner", *Asiaweek*, February 14, 1997, page 55 • Ka-ho Mok and King-yee Wat, "The Merging of the Public and the Private Boundary: Education and the Market Place in China", CUHK, Working Paper 1997/3 • C. Montgomery Broaded and Chongshun Liu, "Family Background, Gender, and Educational Attainment in Urban China", *The China Quarterly*, 145, March 1996: pp.58–86

26 Health

The years of famine aside, China under communism has had a good record on health provision. Better results and better services for the majority was the objective of grassroots training and provision. Since the introduction of the market-led economy, the relationship between financial well-being and health has gone into reverse. The symptoms and causes of this decline in provision is manifold. Rural insurance schemes have collapsed due to the demise of collectives and associated co-operative organizations. So-called barefoot doctors no longer receive workpoints for their service, so now they charge cash. There is a general suspicion of the security of welfare insurance packages, especially in regard to corruption.

Using the most reliable indicator of general health standards, infant mortality, the World Health Organization finds that although there was a vast improvement between 1960 and 1985 (173 per 1,000 to 44 per 1,000), this subsequently worsened to 44.5 in 1990. The indication is that the poorest are suffering. Women in rural areas have a less than one in two chance of getting a post-natal check-up. 77 percent of babies are born at home, 12 percent at a township medical centre, and 9 percent in hospital. Homebirths are not necessarily problematic; indeed, they can help women avoid the complications and infections of hospital doctor-led birthing practices. However, proximity to hospital is a usual condition of homebirth in developed countries, especially on first deliveries. Given the two-child rural policy, most of the births recorded in these figures will be first births. Meanwhile, however, healthcare spending as a proportion of household expenditure is rising rapidly. Health spending stood at 3.5 percent of GNP in 1994, an increase from 0.9 percent in 1981. It is projected to rise to 10 percent of GNP in 2000 and 25 percent by 2025. The accuracy of the forecast will be determined by China's economic performance in the wake of the Asian crisis of 1998. Although household spending on health has risen in response to different structures of provision, it is also due to a higher standard of living and rising expectations of "good health". Those expectations will fall if the market economy does not deliver continuing and expanding returns to the new middle classes.

China's health system is threatened more directly by the tobacco industry (**Map 27**) and the spread of HIV and AIDS. Health officials claim that most Mainland Chinese infected by HIV are intravenous drug users. In areas such as Yunnan's border territory with Burma, on the edge of the "Golden Triangle" of Asian drug production, infection rates are estimated at anywhere between 30 and 70 percent . If it is true that drug users are the most vulnerable in China to AIDS/HIV, then the worst affected area will be in the south. The Health Ministry claims that around 80 percent of users in Guangdong and Guangxi are injecting, compared with 1 percent of users in Shaanxi and Inner Mongolia.

Other vulnerable groups are not being targeted in education or health campaigns. The homosexual population is ignored in government literature, so adequate analyses of sexual behaviours are not available. In a survey in 1995 it was found that 5 percent of rural health clinics re-used needles. Syphilis is spreading and that brings with it increased risks of infection. Professional blood donors are a serious problem. And last but not least, the management of all contagious and infectious diseases is hampered by the movement of the population in search of work. With the high costs of HIV testing in a privatizing health market contemporary disease poses great threats to the financially and sexually disadvantaged in China.

Sources: Yunniu Wu, "Trends and Opportunities in China's Health Care Sector", Murdoch University: Asia Research Centre Policy Paper, no 18. (1997) • "Household Consumption and Market Prospects in China", Murdoch University, Asia Research Centre (1996) • *China Development Briefing*, Issue 4, January 1997 • October 1996 Speech by Chen Minzhang (Health Minister), in *Zhongguo xingbing aizhibing fangzhi zazhi* reported on US Embassy Beijing, http:www.redfish.com

27 Tobacco

It is no secret that tobacco companies in developed countries, faced with a significant decline in smoking, anti-tobacco legislation and lawsuits, anti-tobacco movements and aggressive public hostility towards smokers, are targeting the newly industrialized countries. China beckons, with its huge population, market-oriented economy, impressive economic growth rate, rising living standards, difficulties in enforcing legislation and a thriving tobacco culture in which 70 percent of men smoke. The irony is that, according to a national survey carried out in 1997, while non-smokers are aware of the risks of smoking, the smokers themselves are either not aware of the anti-smoking arguments or, if addicted, reject them. Over 50 percent of Chinese people believe that smoking does little or no harm, more than 60 percent are unaware of its relation to lung cancer and 96 percent do not know that it can cause heart disease.

The map shows the medical, economic and political consequences of smoking. Health officials are acutely aware of the risks for China's 320 million smokers, and the market inroads that foreign brands are making as fashion icons or by being cheap and available as smuggled items. Their position has been strengthened by the publication in 1998 of the biggest study ever undertaken into deaths from tobacco. Scientists from the USA, the UK, and China investigated 1 million deaths and concluded that if current smoking uptake rates persist in China tobacco will kill about 100 million males currently under the age of 29. Half of these deaths will occur in middle age and half in old age.

Even so, this warning may not be enough to induce government action. As anti-tobacco campaigner Judith Mackay observed in 1997, "the biggest cigarette company in the world is the Chinese government not Philip Morris." China produces more tobacco than any other country in the world and the China National Tobacco Corporation, with about 180 factories, is a state monopoly. Tobacco contributes more than 10 percent to total government revenue and, although health costs may outweigh this, tobacco production is too closely integrated into the state economy for it to be easily unscrambled.

Health officials and anti-tobacco campaigners, for example the China Association on Smoking and Health (CASH), have had their triumphs. A 1995 law banned tobacco advertising on radio, television and in print. Since then, smoking has been forbidden in public places in 82 cities. Enforcement, however, has been uneven; loopholes in the laws have been discovered, and where the bans have clashed with the government's other priorities, the latter have prevailed. For example, Formula One motor racing has been given the go-ahead, which means that tobacco advertising on billboards will reach a wide audience. British American Tobacco, producers of 555 cigarette brands, sponsor the traditional dragon-boat race which takes place at 5.00pm on the fifth day of the fifth Chinese lunar month.

The party-state's priority – political stability – means that further legislation and effective enforcement is unlikely for the foreseeable future. An increase in taxes may alienate smokers and encourage even more smuggling and the government has no wish to add to the serious unemployment problem by laying off any of the tobacco industry's 300,000 workforce.

Sources: Chinese Academy of Preventative Medicine, et al, *Smoking and Health in China: 1996: National Preventative Survey of Smoking Patterns*, Beijing, China Science and Technology Press, 1997 • Judith Mackay, *International Herald Tribune*, August 28, 1997 • Liu, Bo-Qi, et al, "Emerging Tobacco Hazards in China: 1. Retrospective proportional mortality study of one million deaths," *British Medical Journal*, vol. 317, November 21, 1998 • *Far Eastern Economic Review*, November 26, 1998

28 Welfare

As the China Human Development Report (1998) notes: "Nothing is more important to China's successful transition to a market economy than the completion of a national social insurance program to cope with unemployment, retirement and health needs of the urban population." The Chinese government is acutely aware of this, not only to meet human needs, but to maintain political stability to which it accords the highest priority.

The economic reforms produced considerable pressures upon the existing welfare services. As the market grew more competititve, the state enterprises found it difficult to carry the burden of their own welfare provisions, including the pensions for their retired workers and support for an over-sized workforce. State-sector employees have also been resistant to losing their employment rights, creating an obstacle to reform. Furthermore, as Gordon White argued, the impact of the economic reforms on the distribution of power has made it difficult for central government to implement a uniform welfare system, even though this has allowed for local flexibility and experimentation. Most important of all have been the demographic changes. The combination of the one-child-family policy and the increase in longevity has had a profound impact on dependency ratios, as the map emphasizes.

Creating a nationwide social insurance system is an immense undertaking. Working in China's favor is its high rate of economic growth, the tradition of family responsibility for the elderly in the countryside, where 70 percent of the population resides, and the decision to delay dismantling the state-owned pillar industries (**Map 8**).

Yet these factors provide no more than a breathing space, and the difficulties in institutionalizing social welfare outweighs them. The first difficulty is the sheer numbers involved and the need for accurate statistical data. The second is the high cost of such an operation and problem of finding funding. The map illustrates the burdens imposed on employed workers by the need to support retired workers.

The third difficulty is that unemployment is likely to be a permanent feature of China's economy. This is compounded by the need to incorporate the mobile population into the welfare system. Fourthly, there is the transition gap. The government has to maintain the existing pensions systems, which are increasingly underfunded. Some schemes have to meet the costs for retired workers with limited personal savings because of low wages, while other schemes benefit workers out of proportion to their earnings. Where the new system has been established for state workers, the evidence suggests that the funds have to be used to support current pensioners. One suggestion has been to extend current insurance coverage beyond the state sector. These firms, however, may prefer to have their own plans, rather than subsidize the state sector.

The fifth difficulty is that care has to be taken not to swell the already large numbers of urban poor. This underlines the need for all-encompassing social insurance and for providing an adequate standard of living. Finally, these factors singularly impact on political stability and collectively threaten it.

The objectives of pension reforms have been to shift responsibility away from the enterprises; to share contributions between the workers, enterprises and the state; to include current and future pensioners; and to establish a system that is effective, efficient and fair. The new pension system involves all cities establishing private accounts for every worker into which the worker and the firm pay. They also pay into pooled contingency funds for such eventualities as a firm being unable to meet its pension responsibilities. According to a spokesperson for the Ministry of Labor, 78 percent of the total urban workforce had joined pension insurance schemes by the end of 1996.

Sources: United Nations Development Programme (UNDP), *China Human Development Report*, 1998 • Gordon White, "Social Security Reforms in China: towards an East Asian model" in Roger Goodman et al (eds) *The East Asian Welfare Model*, London and New York: Routledge 1998 • Linda Wong, *Marginalization and Social Welfare in China*, London and New York: Routledge 1998

29 Religion

Religions are particular systems of faith and worship associated with philosophical explanations of the meaning of life and humanity in particular. Some religions emphasize the magical-sacred, others concentrate on the powers of the living to control existence in appropriate ways. In China there are several ways of understanding religious practise. Household gods and ancestor worship lie at the core of much ritual, although since the founding of the People's Republic in 1949 folk festivals have not been part of the official calendar of national events. Popular Taoism (Daoism) works alongside folk beliefs, local gods and village- or household-centered worship, and is therefore successful and popular. Philosophical Taoism, on the other hand, is concerned with the loss of corporeal signs as motivation in the development of the spirit. Buddhism, and particularly the desire for nirvana, is antithetical to Taoist conceptions of immortality. Christianity and Islam offer a completely different system again, with a focus on a single "true" God, even though each religion disagrees on the nature and commandments of Godliness.

These four are the categories of social and spiritual organization that are generally deemed "religious" in the Chinese context. In Taiwan, the majority are Buddhists, with a strong influence from Japanese/Chinese schools (Zen/Ch'an). The percentages are: Buddhist 22.8; Taoist 18.1; I-Kuan tao 4.4; Christian 3.4; Other 3.3. In Mainland China the majority of believers are Taoist, there are a substantial number of Buddhists, and a smaller number of Muslims and Christians. Many of the Muslims are based in the large minority areas in the west, although there are Muslim communities in Eastern cities also. Muslim religious clothing and schools were becoming visible in Beijing during the late 1990s.

There are other quasi-religious features of Chinese social life which inflect the basic patterns of belief. Confucian rationality and virtue ethics have been out of fashion since 1949, but it is arguable that the connections between virtue and rationality have continued as a feature of politico-philosophical life. The key words of revolutionary discourse, for example, function similarly to the sacred words of religious texts. Timothy Cheek, a scholar of the revolution, points out that "Confucius held that if names were not correct and realities did not conform to correct names, then the moral state would be an impossibility. The Chinese Communist Party exhibits a faith in the power of names similar to that attributed to Confucius". Their use shapes the meaning of everyday life, by giving it an extra dimension, which must be supported by the belief of speaker and, ideally, of listener. It is the communication of belief that occurs in sacred rites and political rallies that brings the concept of religion close to both that of revolution, and to practical political philosophy.

The bête noire of Chinese religious politics is the Tibetan question. Human rights activists draw on both the right to freedom of religion as well as the desire for autonomy in their defence of Tibetan independence. The Chinese government argues that religion is not a sufficient reason for dividing national territory. There is also a problem where religion and ethnicity come together in a nexus of traditonal racisms. Interestingly, despite the Chinese governments criticism of the figure of the Dalai Lama as a cipher of superstition and feudalism, images of Mao Zedong now appear in village temples and urban fetishism. Where before it was the figure and words of Mao that offered a politico-sacred text to his people, now it is his enshrined memory that encapsulates the ancient and the modern in the Chinese religious consciousness. His nirvana is on the earth that made him.

Sources: Timothy Cheek, "The Names of Rectification: Notes on the Conceptual Domains of CCP Ideology in the Yan'an Rectification Movement" in "Keywords of the Chinese Revolution: The Language of Politics and the Politics of Language in 20th-Century China," funded by the National, Endowment for the Humanities and the Pacific Cultural Foundation.
<http://www.easc.indiana.edu/>, or hard copy: Indiana University Press•
James D Seymour, "What The Agenda Has Been Missing", in Susan Whitfield (ed) After the Event: Human Rights and their Future in China, London: Wellsweep, 1993 • Australia Tibet Council News, December 1998 • Journal of Chinese Philosophy, December 1998, vol. 25, nos 1–4 • E. B. Morris, "Philosophic and Religious Content of Chinese Folk Religion," Chinese Culture: A Quarterly Review vol. XXXIX, no. 2, June 1998, pp.1–2.8

30 Telecommunications

The concept of globalization is not new. Cross-border trade, migrations and large-scale interdependencies have long ensured that world communities must sometimes work together. The change in the nature of globalization lies in the collapse of time and space in the wake of advanced systems of communication. Access to the telephone, together with a developed system of web access, is fundamental to power and success in late 20th century international trade and politics. China has been working in support of a socialist market-led economy to modernize its telecommunications infrastructure systems across the territory. Most provincial capitals are now linked by fibre-optic cabling. Cellular phone use and roaming services are expanding to accommodate remote users as well as urban customers. By 2001 China is expected to have a phone line for every ten people. By 2000 China will have five times as many phones per person as India.

The internet in China is provided through educational and government-sponsored establishments. The three top providers are CERNET (China Education and Research Network), CSTNET (China Science and Technology Network), and CHINANET (public service). China has access to 10 percent of the world's available database systems, but the capacity of this data is only 1 percent of total global capacity. Only CHINANET, based in Shanghai and Beijing, is open to general use, and it suffers from a shortage of information storage and access. Users are also restricted by regulations which involve registration with local public security bureaus. "Firewalls" are put in place by domestic and international providers to block access to undesirable sites. However, there are improvements for less-advantaged users in remote areas. Costs of email accounts fell by 800 percent in 1997, a move which gives succor to business and education sectors who operate way outside the coastal mainstream. The overall PC market slowed from 40–60 percent growth to 13.9 percent in 1998, but mostly at the expense of foreign imports. As is true with much electronic equipment, domestic companies are gaining the edge over the market leaders. The domestic PC industry has achieved a steady growth rate of 40 percent since 1994. There are variations here though; in 1997 the sales went up by 66.7 percent, in 1998 that fell to 16.6 percent. This suggests that PC use is not likely to surge across all sectors of the community in the immediate future, but will continue to be concentrated amongst education workers and high-income groups (over $US120 per month). However, forecasters assume that the Chinese concern with education will push web use and digital technology onto centre stage for the next generation, whatever the risks to political conformity.

Sources: Asiaweek, June 20.1997.page 10 • Alysha Webb "Operating with a net", Asiaweek, March 14, 1997 • "On-Line in Yunnan", Asiaweek, May 9th 1997, pp. 48–50 • The South China Morning Post, 18.03.1990, as in • <http://www.technologypost.com/pers> <http://www.virtualchina.com/> • Anura Goonasekera and Duncan Holaday, Asian Communication Handbook, Singapore: Asian Media Information and Communication Centre, 1998 <http://www.redfish.com/USEmbassy-China/sandt/>.

31 Media

The growth of media output and consumption in China is the phenomenal result of a large population, a new-found commitment to consumerism, and the relatively cheap costs of domestic hardware. The media can be described according to the delivery systems which carry the product. Radio, print media (newspapers, magazines), television (cable, terrestrial and satellite), films (delivered through cinema), video (and compact video-disks), and the Internet. Often, however, the term "media" is confused with the product carried by these systems. The question for China, as elsewhere to differing degrees, is the extent to which media systems invite certain types of product. Can media-product be controlled and manipulated by audience taste, cultural specificities, and state interests (whether or not these are mutually compatible)? This is a quandary that is manifested in the State's compulsion to regulate content, or, where that is seen to be impossible, to limit it.

One of the reasons why it might be not just useless but also unnecessary for the government to restrict viewing is the extent to which media delivery is compromised by commercial negotiation. Rules are in place and increasing, but in the meantime long-term arrangements with international media packagers are being developed which exclude dangerous material at source. The Internet still poses a challenge to regulation and the Chinese government has responded with criminal punishments and fines of up to 15,000 yuan (US$1,800) for those who access or provide pornography, anti-Government dissent, political propaganda, amorality and so on. The list is open-ended and gives the authorities plenty of scope for interpretation according to the priorities of the moment. Regulations are also in place for the monitoring and censorship of other media. One cannot publish photographic essays on the lives or work of national figures, alive or dead. Official biographies are authorised, in print and on film, and are tightly monitored for content according to the political line at the time of release. There are also firm controls on the numbers and titles in the publication and distribution of foreign works, and on the release of foreign movie titles.

Most Chinese use their televisions to watch local programs, national news bulletins, and "specials". Long-running serials (soap operas) are also extremely popular. In 1978 China had 32 television stations and 3 million TV sets. Now there are 951 television stations plus 729 cable stations, beamed to over 300 million TV sets, an audience of over 1 billion, and some 55,500 hours of programing per week.

At present all legal media outlets – and all of the terrestrial television stations – are government sponsored. Nevertheless, these stations have needed to purchase international programing in order to compete with one another, and to fill their schedules. In the future it is hoped that CCTV (China Central Television) will be able to move in the other direction, by upgrading their products for foreign sale. At present, much children's programing is bought in from Japan, but there are plans to sell Chinese versions of well-known classics (*Monkey*, *The Water Margin*) in animated TV format. It is already possible to receive satellite TV from China (CCTV 3 and CCTV 4) in 70 countries worldwide.

China's film industry has also received a great deal of attention in the last 15 years (since the release of Chen Kaige's *Yellow Earth* in 1984). The international success of Chinese films by Chen Kaige and Zhang Yimou, known generally as the "Fifth generation" has inspired co-productions between mainland studios and off-shore producers. These co-productions are often better distributed internationally that in the home market. Thus Tian Zhuangzhuang's 1993 film *The Blue Kite* (co-produced between Japan and China) is known to audiences everywhere but in China itself. *Titanic* (1997) is, meanwhile, a hugely successful import, with copies of the film available on compact video-disk, and the theme song playing everywhere from retail shops to television specials.

The reform emphasis on consumer culture in China has led to the concomitant development of advertising. In the wake of the Hong Kong hand-over this is taking on a transnational aspect. One agency holds the franchise for all transport advertising in the 12 major cities. It bases its campaign strategies on Hong Kong successes. Thus, the buses and underground transport systems are getting the environmental uniformity which used to be associated with political posters, but with captions and characters derived from other Asian consumers in an era of multinational capitalism.

Perhaps the clearest observation to make from all this is that the media sphere in China is complicated. On the one hand, much of the media is regulated, and owned, by the Government, and managed in the interests of the State. On the other, delivery diversification, in particular satellite, cable and the Internet, continues to open up possibilities for local programing and wider audience choice. International trade does not automatically lead to a "free press", in fact it may connive against it for commercial advantage. Nevertheless, audience and programme makers are likely to use new systems as well as greater diversity of product to inspire and facilitate "reform and resistance".

Sources: James Lull, *China Turned On: Televison, Reform and Resistance*, London: Routledge, 1991 • Anura Goonasekera and Duncan Holaday, *Asian Communication Handbook*, Singapore: Asian Media Information and Communication Centre, 1998• <http://www.ccnet.com> • <http://www.ccnet.com/> • Annabelle Sreberny-Mohammadi, Dwayne Winseck, Jim McKenna, Oliver Boyd-Barrett, *Media in Global Context*, London: Edward Arnold, 1997

32 Air Pollution

Air pollution is a major threat to health in China. Various factors combine to threaten the atmosphere outside and indoors. Rapid industrialization in a relatively under-capitalized economy leads to environmentally disastrous short-cuts. A population eager to modernize is willing to compromise on air quality, although long-term effects are likely to undermine immediate material gains.

Pollution is increased by an over-capacity of fossil fuel power plants, even in areas expecting to use hydro-electric power in the near future. (**Map 33**). One explanation for this over capacity is localized short-term productivity gains. The power plants look good, on paper at least, in comparison to other smaller industrial enterprises. They thereby enhance the political reputation and financial standing of local officials. Local plants also work to exclude the state power grid, thus producing more income for local businesses, and higher prices for consumers. Electricity costs fluctuate wildly from province to province and county to county.

A casual regard for air quality results in part from the anarchy in nationwide electricity controls. Corrupt local practises have been targeted by Premier Zhu Rongxi in an attempt to protect China's economy and ecology from collapse. He has a tough job ahead of him. Coal-smoke is the major pollutant in Chinese cities, causing smog in certain weather conditions. Outside the cities, the effects of fossil-fuel use are exacerbated by a loss of forest cover. Forests in Sichuan and Jiangsu have been decimated since the 1950s, and forest cover along the Yangtze dropped by over 50 percent in the last 30 years.

Rural and urban indoor pollution is also noted by Chinese scientists. The main causes are fossil-fuel stoves (some without flues), and inadequate ventilation, especially in winter. These dangers acutely affect women working at home during the day. High tobacco usage also pollutes living spaces. The government is not unaware of these problems. The Ministry of Agriculture has improved access to safer stoves, and the Beijing City Council attempted to clean up city air by abolishing high-emission taxi-cabs in 1998. Traffic pollution is not yet at the risk levels of other European and Asian cities, but the typical progression from low car volume to increased high-emission traffic is already indicated in the largest conurbations. There are, however, encouraging signs of Chinese resolve to address the problem, namely plans to merge China'a 160 car manufacturers in order to promote and produce better-quality vehicles, and a decision by Shanghai City Council to sell only lead-free petrol from the end of 1997.

Source: People's Daily, August 17, 1998 and September 25 1998 • <http://www.usembassy-china.gov/english/sandt/> • Song Ruijin, Wang Guifang, Zhou Jinpeng, "Study on the personal exposure level to nitrogen dioxide for housewives in Beijing" in J. J. K. Kaakkola et al (eds), Indoor Air 93: Sixth International Conference on Indoor Air Quality and Climate, vol. 3, pp. 337–42, Helsinki University of Technology, 1993 • Wang Jin and Y. Zhang , "CO2 and particle pollution of indoor air in Beijing and its elemental analysis," Biomedical and Environmental Sciences, vol. 3, pp. 132–38, 1990 • R. Smith Kirk, Gu Shuhua, Kun Huang, Qiu Daxiong, "One hundred million improved cookstoves in China: How was it done?" World Development, vol. 21, no. 6, pp. 941–61, 1993 • Shanghai Newsletter, August 9, 1997 <http://www.shanghai-ed.com/>

33 Water

The monumental Three Gorges dam was planned as a 17-year project (1993–2009). The idea was developed to deal with flooding problems, facilitate water-borne transport systems, and to provide hydro-electric power. The dam was initially suggested in 1919 by Sun Yat-sen, the founding President of Republican China. Only recently have the political will and capital been available for such an enormous undertaking. The former Premier and present Chairman of the Standing Committee of the National People's Congress, Li Peng, has staked his reputation on it.

There are, however, big questions surrounding China's major and hugely ambitious development in water management. They concern the migration and resettlement of local populations, the quality of the project design, and the eventual cost of power in the aftermath of the project. As building continues, the areas around the flooded sites are over-crowded and ecologically unsustainable. It is feared that unless migration is speeded up to match the pace of construction, there will be problems in land management. Archaeological concerns are also being raised. The dam is costing China 30 million RMB every day, but little of this money has gone towards protecting historical relics in the region (1 percent of 1.9 billion RMB). It is projected that at this rate only 20 percent of the relics will be preserved.

Many of these worries have been taken up by central government, particularly the question of the quality of the design. The Finance Minister, Zhu Rongji, has warned against "speed at all costs," and is monitoring progress accordingly. The dam is the overwhelming example of the modernization of China's infrastructure. It is vital that corruption, shoddy workmanship, and poor management do not undermine the sustainability of China's long-term economy and the well-being of local populations. The Yangtze floods of 1998 reminded China of the horrors and cost of water damage, and also pointed up the problems of poor construction standards and non-ecologically motivated planning. More generally, water conservancy nationwide is being targeted to reduce corruption; up to 1.39 billion RMB was found to have been siphoned off to inappropriate projects in nineteen provinces investigated over the past couple of years.

Source: "Japan MITI evaluates Three Gorges Dam Project" • <http://www.redfish.com/USEmbassy-China/sandt> • "Infrastructure Project Quality Reports Due March 31" <http://www.chinadaily.com> • <http://www.usembassy-china.gov/english/sandt> • People's Daily December 21, 1998

34 Biodiversity

Apologists for the increasing number of endangered species in newly industrializing countries such as China point to the need for economic growth. Population pressures, food production and limited resources steer government priorities towards meeting immediate demands and needs, and away from consideration of longer term consequences. This approach, however, no longer stands up to analysis.

In the first place, biodiversity is universally recognized as an issue for industrialized as well as industrializing countries. Secondly, biodiversity as a global issue is no longer subscribed to simply out of enlightened concern, but is seen as a matter of naked self-interest and human survival. The protection and conservation of animals, plants and insects, once understood in the context of the food chain, for example, become priorities.

Thirdly, China wants to be counted in the global club of international environmental agreements and conventions. This is in part the result of its policies of reform and opening up. It is also due to the worldwide and emotive publicity given to China's giant panda. Most of all, perhaps, the lessons of biodiversity have been learned the hard way, as deforestation has been a major cause of devastating floods, severe droughts and serious soil erosion (**Map 33**). The Worldwide Institute in Washington, for example, estimated that 85 percent of the forests in the Yangtse river basin have disappeared. The Yellow River has had dry periods since 1985 and no water reached the sea for 226 days in 1997. Soil erosion is taking place throughout the world at an alarming rate and in China contributes to the continuing decline to its already limited arable land.

While the decline in the variety of China's animal and plant life has been a long-term process, the reform and open policies have had an adverse, as well as a positive, effect. The trade in rare species, that was once limited to domestic consumption, is now on the world market. The trade in tiger body parts, for example, may be illegal under the Convention on International Trade in Endangered Species and China prohibits their sale but those who wish to indulge in tiger penis soup can do so for a price.

Source: press reports

35 Unfinished Business

China's century has been extraordinary. In the first 50 years China moved from an Imperial dynastic system besieged by foreign powers, through a republic, the anti-Japanese war and civil war, to Liberation in 1949 under Mao Zedong and the Chinese Communist Party. In the past 50 years there has been land and social reform, famine, the Great Proletariat Cultural Revolution, and now the market-oriented economy. The changes have been dramatic, swift and often unexpected. One needs to be cautious about predicting China's future in the 21st century.

At the Thirteenth National Congress of the CCP (September 1997) Jiang Zemin's summation of the past century was divided into three parts, with three heroes: first, Dr Sun Yatsen and the Republican Revolution of 1911; second, Mao Zedong and the founding of the People's Republic of China; third, Deng Xiaoping and the reform era when "our Party reviewed historical experience and lessons and blazed a new trail in building Chinese socialism with Chinese characteristics."

It is the third period which has principally featured in this atlas. Yet many of the issues and conundrums noted in the preceding maps are related to practises developed and sustained in previous eras. To that degree the future may be surmised. Immediate concerns for 1999 and the year 2000 revolve around the state of the Asian economies, and the degree to which Chinese exporters can compete with low-priced exports from countries hit by crisis in 1997 and 1998. It seems certain that China will continue to expand its visibility in virtual industries. China internet users were projected to reach 5.5 million by mid 1999 and 10 million in 2000; a multi-national Cyberport is planned for Hong Kong; mobile phones are now equipped with software that "speaks" Chinese, and Bill Gates, the Microsoft billionaire, has cut a deal in China.

The political future of China is less easy to decipher. Economic reform is coupled with political stability. As the maps indicate, unemployment, corruption and environmental degradation loom large, although there are signs of positive institutional and constitutional development. Sustainable development is also on the agenda, with *China Agenda 21* and the *Trans-Century Green Plan*. China is negotiating to join the World Trade Organization, a move that would further integrate trade and political relations across global ideological systems, but will encounter on-going condemnation of human rights abuses even in the event of progress.

Sources: CINET-L Newsletter Issue no. 102 (CN99-03) March 12,1999 <http://www.cnd.org> • "Jiang Zemin's report at the 15th National Congress of the Communist Party of China" • <http://www.china-embassy.org> • <http://www.insidechina.com/china/newss> • <http://www.chinadaily.net/cndy>

SELECT BIBLIOGRAPHY

Primary sources

Amnesty International, *People's Republic of China: The Death Penalty Log 1997*, London: Amnesty International, September 1998

China Foreign Economic Statistical Yearbook, Beijing: China Statistical Publishing House, 1996

China Labour Statistical Yearbook, Beijing: China Statistical Publishing House, 1997

China Regional Economy: A Profile of 17 Years of Reform and Opening Up, Beijing: China Statistical Publishing House, 1996

China Statistical Yearbook, Beijing: China Statistical Publishing House, various years

China Population Statistics Yearbook, Beijing: China Statistical Publishing House, 1997

China Quarterly various issues

Chinese Academy of Preventive Medicine et al., *Smoking and Health in China 1996*, Beijing: China Science and Technology Press, 1997

Chinese Academy of Social Sciences, *Information China*, New York and Oxford: Pergamon Press, 1989

Economist, May 1997

Far Eastern Economic Review various issues

International Institute of Strategic Studies (IISS), *The Military Balance, 1998/1999*, London: IISS, 1998

International Labour Office, *Yearbook of Labour Statistics 1997*, Geneva: ILO, 1997

National Committee on Aging, *Elderly Populations in China*, Beijing, 1997

Observer Human Rights Index, Observer, London, June 28, 1998

UNESCO, *World Education Report 1998*, Paris: UNESCO, 1998

United Nations Centre for Human Settlements (HABITAT), *An Urbanizing World: Global Report on Human Settlements*, New York: Oxford University Press, 1996

United Nations Development Programme (UNDP), *China Human Development Report*, United Nations,1998

United Nations Development Programme (UNDP), *Human Development Report*, United Nations,1998

US Bureau of the Census, International Data Base, International Programs Center, Washington, D.C., 1998

World Bank, *The Chinese Economy*, Washington: World Bank, 1997

World Bank, *World Bank Atlas*, Washington: World Bank, 1998

World Resources Institute, *World Resources 1998-99*, New York: Oxford University Press, 1998

Secondary sources

Barnett, Robert, ed., *Resistance and Reform in Tibet*, London: Hurst, 1994

Benewick, Robert and Wingrove, Paul, *China in the 1990s*, rev. ed., London: Macmillan; Vancouver: University of British Columbia Press, 1999

Blecher, Marc, *China Against the Tides*, New York: Pinter, 1997

Conway, Gordon, *The Double Green Revolution*, London: Penguin, 1997

Cook, Sarah and Gordon White, *China: A Poverty Profile*, report for the Department of International Development, 1997

Dolven, Ben et. al., "Asia's Car Crush," *Far Eastern Economic Review*, May 5, 1997

Dreyer, June Teufel, *China's Political System: Modernization and Tradition*, 2nd edition, London: Macmillan, 1996

Edmonds, Richard Louis, ed.,"China's Environment," *China Quarterly*, special issue, December 1998

Gittings, John, *Real China: from Cannibalism to Karaoke*, New York: Simon and Schuster, 1996

Goddard, Charles, *China Market Atlas*, London: Economist Intelligence Unit, 1997

Goodman, David S. G., ed., *China's Provinces in Reform*, London and New York: Routledge, 1997

Hoogvelt, Ankie, *Globalisation and the Postcolonial World: The New Political Economy of Development*, London: Macmillan, 1997

Jacka, Tamara, *Women's Work in China: Change and Continuity in an Era of Reform*, Cambridge and Melbourne: Cambridge University Press, 1997

Kidron, Michael and Dan Smith, *The War Atlas*, London and Sydney: Pan Books, 1983

Liu, Bo-Qi, et al., "Emerging Tobacco Hazards in China: Retrospective proportional mortality study of one million deaths," *British Medical Journal*, 317, November 21, 1998

Mackerras, Colin, *China's Minorities*, Hong Kong: Oxford University Press, 1994

Mackerras, Colin, et al., eds., *Dictionary of the Politics of the People's Republic of China*, London and New York: Routledge, 1998

Naisbitt, J., "Megatrends Asia," *Overseas Economy Yearbook*, 1996

Nakai, Y., ed., *China's Road Map*, 15th Party Congress, Tokyo Institute of Developing Economies, 1998

O'Brien, Joanne and Martin Palmer, *The State of Religion Atlas*, New York and London: Simon and Schuster, 1993

Ong, A. and Nonini, D., *Ungrounded Empires: The Cultural Politics of Modern Chinese Transnationalism*, London: Routledge, 1997

Pearson, Ian, ed., *The Atlas of the Future*, New York: Macmillan Inc; London: Routledge, 1998

Saywell, Trish, "A Lease on Life," *Far Eastern Economic Review*, November 26, 1998

Seager, Joni, *The State of Environment Atlas*, New York and London: Penguin, 1995

Seymour, James D. and Anderson, Richard, *New Ghosts, Old Ghosts: Prisons and Labor Reform Camps in China*, Armonk, New York: M. E. Sharpe, 1998

Shambaugh, David, ed, "China's Military in Transition," *The China Quarterly*, special issue, June 1996

Shambaugh, David, ed., *Greater China*, Oxford: Oxford University Press, 1995

Shoesmith, Brian, "No Sex! No Violence! No News!: Satellite and Cable Television in China," *Media in Asia*, 23 (1), 1998

Smith, Dan, *The State of War and Peace Atlas*, London and New York: Penguin, 1997

State Planning Commission, cited in Goddard

Tung, Ricky, "Possible Development of Mainland China's Private Enterprises," *Issues and Studies*, 33 (6), June 1997

White, Gordon, et al, *In Search of Civil Society*, London: Macmillan, 1997

White, Gordon, "Social Security Reforms in China, towards an East Asian model" in Roger Goodman, et al (eds) *The East Asian Welfare Model*, London and New York: Routledge 1998

White III, Lynn T., *Unstately Power: Vol. 1. Local Causes of China's Economic Reforms*, Armonk, New York: M. E. Sharpe, 1998

Wong, L., *Marginalization and Social Welfare in China*, London and New York: Routledge, 1998

Zheng, Shiping, *Party vs State in Post-1949 China*, Cambridge: Cambridge University Press, 1997